A RotoVision Book
Published and Distributed by RotoVision SA
Rue Du Bugnon 7
CH-1299 Crans-Près-Céligny
Switzerland

RotoVision SA, Sales & Production Office
Sheridan House, 112/116A Western Road
Hove, East Sussex BN3 1DD, UK

Tel: +44 (0) 1273 72 72 68
Fax: +44 (0) 1273 72 72 69
e-mail: sales@RotoVision.com
Web: www.RotoVision.com

Distributed to the trade in the United States by:
Watson-Guptill Publications
1515 Broadway
New York, NY 10036
USA

10 9 8 7 6 5 4 3 2 1

ISBN: 2-88046-392-0

Book design by Salisbury Communications

Production and separations in Singapore by ProVision Pte. Ltd.
Tel: +65 334 7720
Fax: +65 334 7721

ART DIRECTOR CONFESSES:

BY MIKE SALISBURY

"I SOLD SEX! Drugs & ROCK'n'ROLL"

For April who had this idea. Terry Lamb who helped make it all happen. Lloyd Ziff, Greg Escalante and Paula Scher who said I did good; Elizabeth who challenged me, Victoria who made me prove I had done famous things and those women like my aunt Fern, that third grade teacher and Barbara Mercer. It's all my grandparents' fault... my mom's dad just wanted me to have a good time... my dad's mom wanted me to know guilt. And thank you Professor Cleary, Jann, Larry Dietz, Joel Siegle, James Bellows, and Otis Chandler.

CONTENTS

My high school was *happy to ge*

Even though I had some of the highest academic scores on their tests, I was rejected by the U.S. Naval Academy. I was kicked out of architecture school. I was fired from one of the biggest ad agencies in the country. In spite of all this, my work has contributed over $200 billion to the American GNP – $100 billion alone just from the Levi's 501 brand name I created. Levi's, a great American brand representing all that is America – the Old World's talents and the New World's needs. Just like me.

My mother's folks came over on the Mayflower. My dad wasn't here that long; he blew into town from Vienna. He left soon after I was born. She was a swing dancer the first time it was popular, and he played poker. I was raised first by a family in San Francisco. The father was a cook in an Italian restaurant. Then mom remarried, to a ramrod naval officer from the Calvinistic Iowa of the great American Midwest. He taught me to read before I ever went to school. His sister was a high school English teacher who taught me to love writing. Other women in my life told me I was observant and talented. My grandfather gave me the gift of fun. Phil Lansdale taught me merchandising, and Hugh Hefner taught me how to have more fun and how to package it. George Lucas collected my work and Francis Coppola created jobs just for me. With a glittery white glove, I created a look for Michael Jackson. I made 'Rolling Stone' look like a real magazine instead of something you rolled joints with. I gave the world's biggest toy company an identity. I have helped sell over 300 movies and I put L.A. pop culture on the map.

My work got Larrry Flynt to the Supreme Court for being sarcastic, and I got my Joe Camel fired for being a dick. I can get attention. Maybe I owe it all to my stepfather. He didn't talk to me much after I became 9 years old. He didn't give me any attention. My mom didn't know how to. I need attention. Attention! Attention shoppers! I just love attention.

In the fifth grade, copying illustrations from the dictionary got me attention. We lived in Hawaii then. My family moved at least once a year. I designed my California high school yearbook and gave myself a printed credit. After that, painting flames and skulls on cars got me attention in Michigan. I went back to California and traded logo designs for surfboards. Those logos are still used today and I am still known for them. Attention surfers! I attended over 20 schools between the first grade and high school graduation. Being the new kid that many times can get you the wrong kind of attention; if I wasn't careful, I could have my ass kicked. I had to sell. I had to sell myself. I learned how to fit in, to find the cultural groove, to learn the local language of communication. A lot of that is in ciphers – fashion, language, custom, protocol-cool. The American vernacular. Cool. Kids' cool. I have never grown up. I'm still 15. That is how I make a living. I talk to the pubescent in puberty. I think I'm cool. I'm too old to get beaten up for saying that now. We all want to be cool. 5, 15, 50 years-old cool is where it is at. Sex, drugs, and rock and roll. Cool. American.

Visualizing also helped me picture in my mind's eye exactly where I wanted to go in life. What I wanted out of school. What I wanted in terms of a career. I could see my goals and visualize my destinations. I could see the steps to get there. I saw it. I got there.

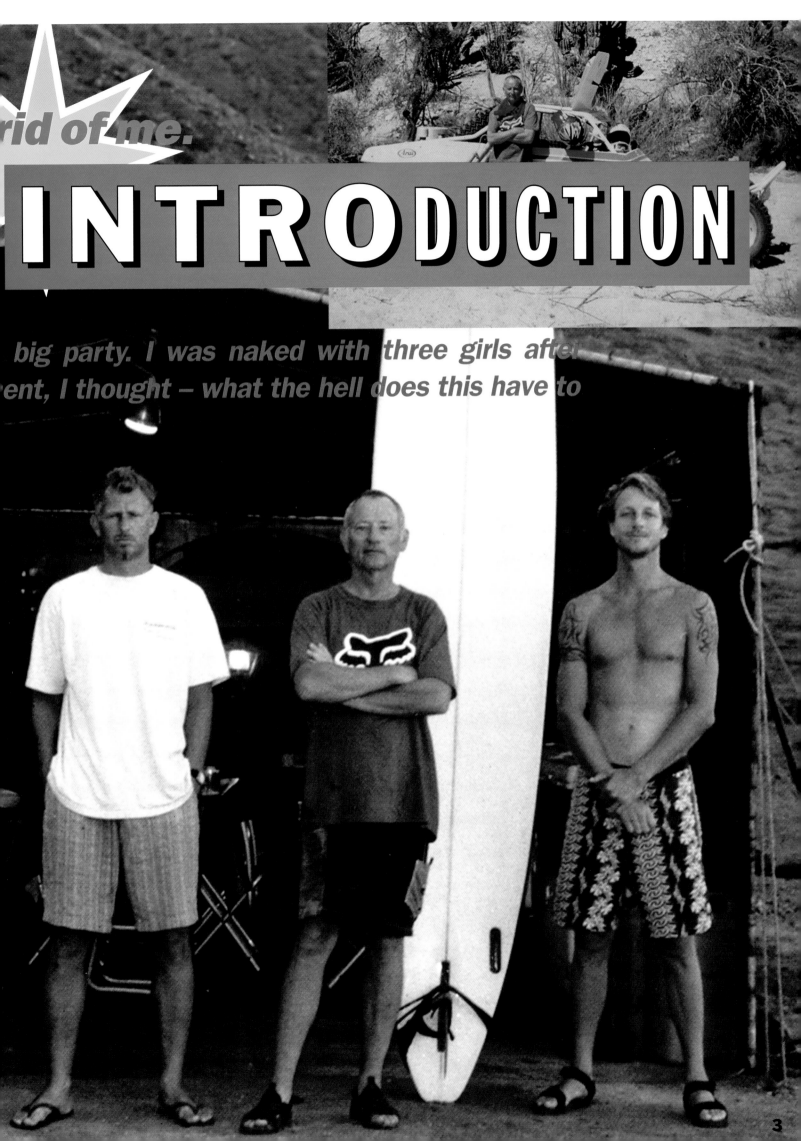

rid of me.

INTRODUCTION

big party. I was naked with three girls after
rent, I thought – what the hell does this have to

I sell cool.

With design for magazines and fashion and movies and games and corporations. With advertising that sells cool by being cool. On TV and in print and with packaging and image creation. I get attention. Cool attention. I get it for my clients. That attention sells goods and services.

All of this coolness is a result of choosing to be in on the popular culture rather than out of it. An ability to sell comes from overcoming shyness. Using design and communication abilities to sell comes from needing instant gratification by trading my work for something I wanted or needed. Decisiveness comes from taking things into my own hands, because my stepfather could not and would not make decisions. Strategic thinking comes from my plotting and scheming little mind. And probably too much time on my hands. I have sold with popular culture – using icons and styles we live with and communicate with non-verbally. I have sold popular culture – toys, movies, pinups, surfing, motorcycles and music. With my contributions to books and magazines I have introduced popular culture to the unaware, through photos and articles on custom cars, pinups, airbrush illustration, Disney art, Coca-Cola memorabilia, Hollywood apartments, tattoos, movie posters, etc. This all was done according to a plan. I didn't have a written document; I just knew where I wanted to go. And I chose the destinations. I wanted to design. I did.

I created logos for international giants like Honda, Hasbro, PolyGram, and entertainment success stories like 'Jurassic Park', 'Raiders of The Lost Ark' and George Lucas's Industrial Light and Magic, packaging for Mattel and Kirin, uniforms, sets, props and even the characters for movies like 'Dick Tracy'. I created what you perceive as the person Marlon Brando played in 'Apocalypse Now'. I designed music covers for George Harrison and Michael Jackson, James Taylor and Ricky Lee Jones, Ry Cooder and Fats Domino. Magazines always were a love of mine and I chose to work in the editorial trades. Live work as an art director, an illustrator, a photographer and a writer. I redesigned 'Rolling Stone', 'Surfing' and 'The San Francisco Examiner'; art directed 'Playboy' and 'Surfer'; I took pictures for 'Time' and 'Esquire' and 'Forbes'. I write for 'Forbes' and 'Rolling Stone's 'Men's Journal'. I illustrated for others. I needed a job after 'Surfer' – I chose advertising. It may have chosen me. I lived at the beach. I did not want to move. The only jobs for designers were in the city. My favourite agency was right in my yard, a few steps from the ocean.

I was hired and given my first professional title – art director. Besides myself there was another illustrator. That artist gave me the best advice I ever had: use ideas. Do not rely on a personal style or pure design to get you through life. People relate to ideas. That job taught me my best lesson for life, a lesson later summed up by my friend and fan Warren Hinckle, another well-known troublemaker in editorial circles: "when you have a lemon, make lemonade." Some of my best known work came from dead-end jobs. Lemons. Jobs no one else would take. Jobs that were not even jobs. I was told before I took the jobs that defined what I do that 'Rolling Stone' was a dirty little paper about sex, drugs and rock and roll. Levi's had already done their best advertising. 'West' magazine could never be anything but a liner for a birdcage, and movie posters, titles and trailers were not real advertising. At those dead-end jobs I learned. And I grew. Because no one cared to watch, I learned while I earned. I became a photographer, a creative director a commercial director, a writer – all on someone else's dime.

After I had developed a professional reputation I was offered the trophy jobs. Frances Coppola hired me to be the art director of his 'City Magazine'. I took the role of precious genius so seriously. I became an *enfante terrible*, firing anyone I wanted to, including the editor. But I also developed people. I made the production artists, all of whom were so loyal, art directors. They were good and responsible. They went on to become major players in design – Diana La Guardia art directed 'The New York Times Magazine', 'Esquire', Conde Naste's 'Traveler' and 'House and Garden'. Roger Carpenter has his own international design practice, and Doug Claybourne, an ex-Marine whom I made into our production manager, became a major film producer because I sold his extraordinary organisational skills to Frances to help him keep 'Apocalypse Now'

Dreeeeeam.
Dream
Dream.

Dream

try all the possibilities. I do it their way. I do it my way. I do it responsively and I do it **strategically.** In other words – I do what the client asks for and I do what I like. I do it top of mind and it to the research."

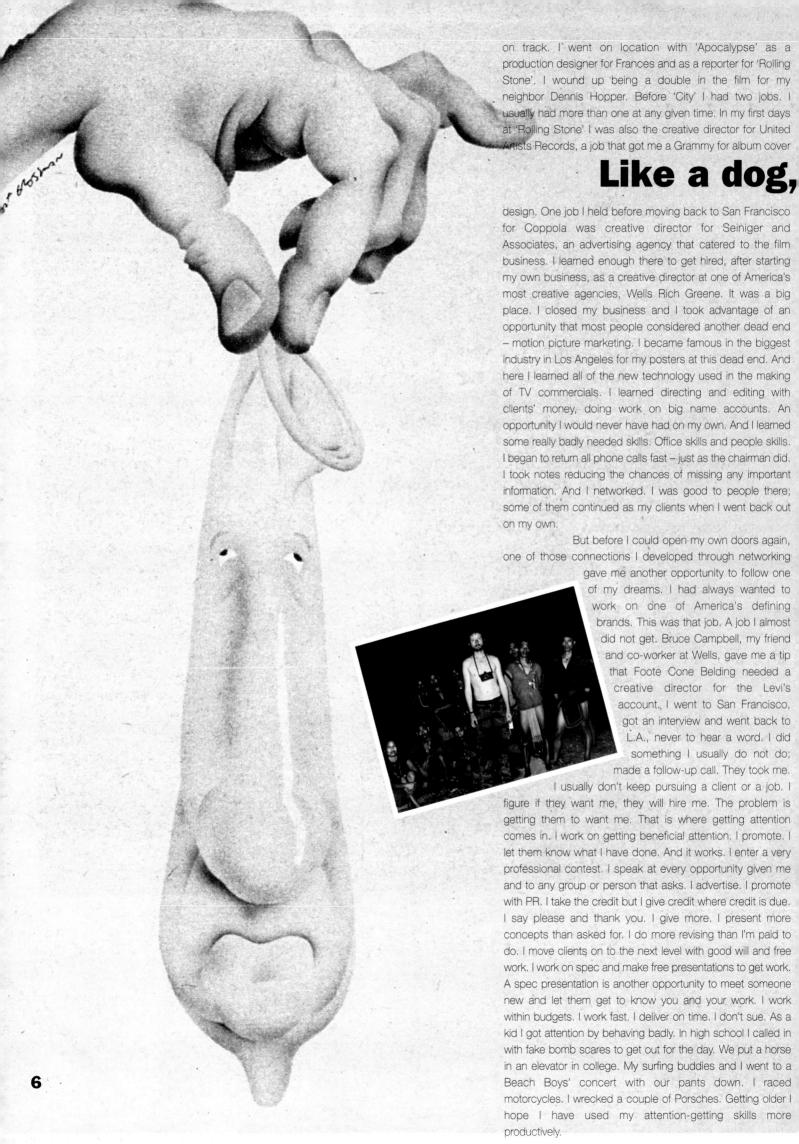

on track. I went on location with 'Apocalypse' as a production designer for Frances and as a reporter for 'Rolling Stone'. I wound up being a double in the film for my neighbor Dennis Hopper. Before 'City' I had two jobs. I usually had more than one at any given time. In my first days at 'Rolling Stone' I was also the creative director for United Artists Records, a job that got me a Grammy for album cover

Like a dog,

design. One job I held before moving back to San Francisco for Coppola was creative director for Seiniger and Associates, an advertising agency that catered to the film business. I learned enough there to get hired, after starting my own business, as a creative director at one of America's most creative agencies, Wells Rich Greene. It was a big place. I closed my business and I took advantage of an opportunity that most people considered another dead end – motion picture marketing. I became famous in the biggest industry in Los Angeles for my posters at this dead end. And here I learned all of the new technology used in the making of TV commercials. I learned directing and editing with clients' money, doing work on big name accounts. An opportunity I would never have had on my own. And I learned some really badly needed skills. Office skills and people skills. I began to return all phone calls fast – just as the chairman did. I took notes reducing the chances of missing any important information. And I networked. I was good to people there; some of them continued as my clients when I went back out on my own.

But before I could open my own doors again, one of those connections I developed through networking gave me another opportunity to follow one of my dreams. I had always wanted to work on one of America's defining brands. This was that job. A job I almost did not get. Bruce Campbell, my friend and co-worker at Wells, gave me a tip that Foote Cone Belding needed a creative director for the Levi's account. I went to San Francisco, got an interview and went back to L.A., never to hear a word. I did something I usually do not do; made a follow-up call. They took me.

I usually don't keep pursuing a client or a job. I figure if they want me, they will hire me. The problem is getting them to want me. That is where getting attention comes in. I work on getting beneficial attention. I promote. I let them know what I have done. And it works. I enter a very professional contest. I speak at every opportunity given me and to any group or person that asks. I advertise. I promote with PR. I take the credit but I give credit where credit is due. I say please and thank you. I give more. I present more concepts than asked for. I do more revising than I'm paid to do. I move clients on to the next level with good will and free work. I work on spec and make free presentations to get work. A spec presentation is another opportunity to meet someone new and let them get to know you and your work. I work within budgets. I work fast. I deliver on time. I don't sue. As a kid I got attention by behaving badly. In high school I called in with fake bomb scares to get out for the day. We put a horse in an elevator in college. My surfing buddies and I went to a Beach Boys' concert with our pants down. I raced motorcycles. I wrecked a couple of Porsches. Getting older I hope I have used my attention-getting skills more productively.

...was waiting for an erection brought on by...

Why?

The real reason? I loved females. I still love them. Moving so much threw me into new situations with new girls. I loved kissing them ever since I took a neighbor into the closet when I was 6. I played doctor so many times I should be an honorary MD. I suppose I learned visualization and salesmanship early, when I tried to imagine myself with the prettiest girl and then worked on meeting her.

Rejection, a major component of this business — like sketching, selling and visualizing — was also an early lesson. In high school, at a monster of a new school about the size of a small city — another one of the great wonder years' experiments, along with thalidomide — my beloved at that time ran off with a guy with a car. So I took out my pain with pranks and work.

It was a new school. Hospital-sterile with Dalmatian-patterned linoleum floors and those flesh-colored metal desks that were always too small and had gum and snot congealed to the underside of a cheap wooden top carved like a high school delinquents' version of a faux Chinese coffee table. I sat in the back of the class near a closet with blonde plywood doors about 8 feet high. Like a dog, I was waiting for an erection brought on by the warm sun and numbing boredom of class to subside, so to kill time I unscrewed the hinges of those closet doors. After I could safely leave my seat in full upright position, I told the class fatty that he left something in those very closets. He thanked me more for giving him some attention than the news, and waddled back into the room to retrieve something he never even had. Skulking, **like Wiley Coyote, with my fingers in my ears, my eyes closed and my back bent over to shield me, I waited for the crash.** It came and I was instantly transported by the ear under the thumb of some school authority to a place where possibly I could rehabilitate myself. It was the yearbook staff offices.

This was 1950s' Southern California. The era of the third Gold Rush after the one of WWII. This was the Jetson's future sponsored by the military industrial complex — the aerospace age. And we were swinging.

Tailfins. Pink and black Calder-inspired graphics. Pastiches of Saarinen architecture. The furniture of Charles Eames and the custom cars of George Barris.

Pegged pants, ducktail haircuts and 'The Nelsons' — Ozzie, Harriet, Ricky and David. **Rock & Roll and that newly-minted class of humans — teenage, juvenile delinquents living in the stucco boredom of pastel-colored housing tracts. And cool.** And I put that yearbook into the age of the drive-in church and the double-deck cheeseburger. I threw away the 'Ye Old English Speedball' lettering. I took a chance. I presented my ideas. I sold them. I was on my way to a career in solving communications problems and taking chances with design. And the girls liked what I had done.

Before this school, I'd moved freshly-scrubbed, freckle-faced and obviously naive from Miami to Lakewood, California. I discovered cool. Well, I discovered you had to be cool to keep from being killed by the cool guys and you had to be cool to get the chicks. My grades were always straight As since I could go to the bathroom and unbutton my pants by myself, but today the authority-person in charge of getting me a seat in classes failed to notice my academic record, and was focusing the lower part of her thick bifocals on a list of the electives I should be dumped off at. Art. "It says here you are good at art" — great, I thought to my little underdeveloped self — the queer classes.

'Jann Wenner asked me to join him in his Jacuzzi... I kept sober. I kept quiet. I kept my pants on.,,

SAGA

2

THROWN OUT OF SCHOOL FOR IDEAS AND BOMB THREATS

GETTING INTO TROUBLE WITH ART AND DESIGN

I didn't know printing was art but being called a printer sounded better to me than faggot artist, as my first brother-in-law would later call me. I pushed open the grimy door of the print shop on that warm yellowy day of suburban California heat and saw what looked like from that distance, my little classmates being responsible apprentices. With the help of the shop teacher — a little guy in shirtsleeves and a tie tucked away from the grease and ink under his buttons so he could wear it again, and again — I was silently shown a stool to sit on and a type stick to put the little backwards metal letters into. Now learning why we call it upper- and lower-case type was ultimately much more important but not as impressive as seeing the knives being made out of the metal type sticks by boys who looked less like Tom Swift, Boy Printer and more like pimply-faced midget versions of The Ramones.

I didn't make a knife, but I did learn when I could find enough letters to do so, how to create words in type and print them on a letterpress. I also saw my first joint held proudly aloft like Liberty's torch as the only bright light that could squeeze out of the smog. I was just 12. But I didn't inhale. Not then at least. I just wasn't cool enough yet.

My introduction to how to be cool came from a classmate at that Lakewood Junior High who wore a pink little skinny belt with the buckle off to one side. It wrapped around his Levi's which were never ever washed and had the baggy legs hanging with the ribboned cuffs about two inches above white suede shoes that laced up the sides. Rocky wore his collar up on a turquoise blue gabardine windbreaker with saddle stitching over a mandarin collar shirt of yellow gingham check. His mother was an unacceptable species — a single mom. A lesbian who rode a Harley and answered to the name of Billy. Cool.

Like today, we had niche cultural groups of kids — tribes. We had the hipsters like Rocky but we had the soshes, the jocks and the hoods. And we had Ivy Leaguers too. Button-down Madras plaid shirts and khaki pants. Flat top haircuts that were short enough on top to see skin, but left long on the sides Like Ricky Nelson. Jivy Ivy. And they had to have foreign cars.

Frosty Myers dropped out of that school and eventually went to work in Andy Warhol's factory. In school he shoplifted enough from the right stores to be Ivy. He looked like Ricky Nelson. His mom was single too, but instead of motorcycles she had foreign cars. She had the first VW bug, the first Volvo P44. She smoked, and drank and dated men. She wasn't like any other mom. She looked as straight as June Cleaver but she was cool. Like Billy, she talked to us kids like we were people in those days when we were supposed to be seen and not heard — like furniture. Frosty stole her cars and we went joy riding — stuffing as many of our moron friends into those little vehicles as we could. We were cool. That was all way too cool. That was 1957. The year of the Chevy and 'Don't Be Cruel'. The year Elvis came to sing in my town. The first year I even liked Elvis. After Rocky, before Elvis, my taste was the cooler R&B music on my Philco radio from The Huggy Boy Show. The hard core blues and doo-wop of Huntin' With Hunter.

In 1957 pinstriping and flame designs were happening on hot rods and custom cars. Frosty and I learned how to pinstripe by ruining our mock colonial era bedroom furniture from Sears, our precious Schwinn bicycles and his mom's little foreign cars. 1957 was also the year my family moved away to Michigan. I took my idea of cool with me.

Walking to the first day of school on a quiet Michigan September Monday warmed all over like an electric blanket by an orange sun just above the first fog of autumn, my cool just about got my ass kicked.

Just like I learned from life experience the tools I would later need to pursue my career; handling rejection, visualization, drawing and selling, I was now going to learn a big lesson for being a professional in the creative services industry. I was going to learn how to see the other person's view of things. I was going to learn to fit in. To adapt. To fucking survive.

A car of no particular interest to a cool guy like me wobbled past, chugging along in the same direction as mine. Inside I saw a bunch of light-colored heads of very short hair. Someone hostile yelled at me from an open window and I responded in kind — like the wanna-be tough guy I was. I thrust the air above my head with a stab of my middle finger. Well shit, you could smell the burnin' rubber as they hit the brakes and ripped it into reverse.

Looking like a small Marine Corps, the entire front line of the high school football team I was on my way to be a classmate of jumped out of that sedan. It did not take me long to ask where I could get one of those really neat haircuts, after I swore I was only waving them down to do just that. I asked to pre-empt their needs. To get into their heads. To serve them. Like I would for any client, I showed them my idea of what I thought worked — by looking cool in my way. They had a different plan for me. And much like listening to a client's idea of what may be right, I listened. And I got that haircut, I fitted in. I survived to fight another day. I worked on that school's yearbook too and I did other cool stuff in my way. I did my things like my drawing and my humor, and I got the girls while fitting in for the guys.

In the summer after graduating from high school, the summer of 'Dream, Dream, Dream' by the Everly Brothers, that first summer on my own — I started my first business. Well, actually my second. I sold flower seeds and greeting cards door-to-door to get a camera when I was 6. This was my first creative business. I travelled the state to car shows and drag races and I made money doing something cool. Something I taught myself. I painted flames and pinstriping on cars. I learned to charge fairly against my mother's advice that I was selling myself too cheaply. I learned not to give half of what you make to the person who only bought the equipment I created with. And I learned how to overcome objections.

Flaming a car means that just like a shoe on one foot matches the shoe on the other foot, the design painted on the car must be the same on each side. It is a long process. You first design the overall flame pattern that works best to the car's design and to what the owner might want. Then you raw the design onto the car in outline with a crayon. Tape, very narrow masking tape, is applied along the crayon line as a trap for the paint you will spray in layers of fire colors. The area of the car not being flamed is masked off with newspaper. After the flames are painted, the entire outline is traced in paint with a very thin little brush called a striping dagger. Once both sides are completed you have to clean up the whole mess.

We were very busy that summer with our little business. We were the first to bring the California cool of car painting to Michigan, my overpaid partner and I. I never had a payment collection problem. I always delivered. I painted both sides to match.

Except once. It was the end of a long weekend of designing, stooping, painting and cleaning up. It was a hot and humid Midwestern afternoon. My fingers were stuck together with dried paint. I was falling asleep at the airbrush. I was hungry. I was shot. I finished a beautiful design on the side of a lowered black Mercury coupé. The car James Dean had in 'Rebel Without A Cause'.

A sleepwalker. Tiredly trudging through time, I pulled off the paper and unraveled the tape. I was all stuck up in a big ball of sticky crap like a fly in a web. I wrote up an invoice on my little pad and handed it over to my perplexed client. He looked up from the little blue striped piece of paper torn from its spiral binding and whimpered, "what about the other side?" "What other side?" barely slobbered out of the side of my dry mouth. "Do you read the cool custom car magazines?" I managed to ask. "Well yeah — I see them". "Well", I asked in my haughtiest tone like the artiste I was, "ever see two pictures, two sides of a flame-painted car in the magazines?" "Well, no. Now I don't really recall seeing but one side of a car with flames in the magazines". With my eyes closed and my hand out, I whispered close to his ear, "that is the way it is my friend". On the barrel-head. He pulled the greenbacks out of his jeans, paid his bill in full and drove off to show his friends at the F.F.A. grange his slick California-cool flame job on the left side there please.

Bingo!

I overcame an objection. I closed my deal. I got off the hook. I had myself a nice shower and dinner and fell asleep on someone's couch with a somewhat guilty conscience, but knowing I had been a real businessman that day.

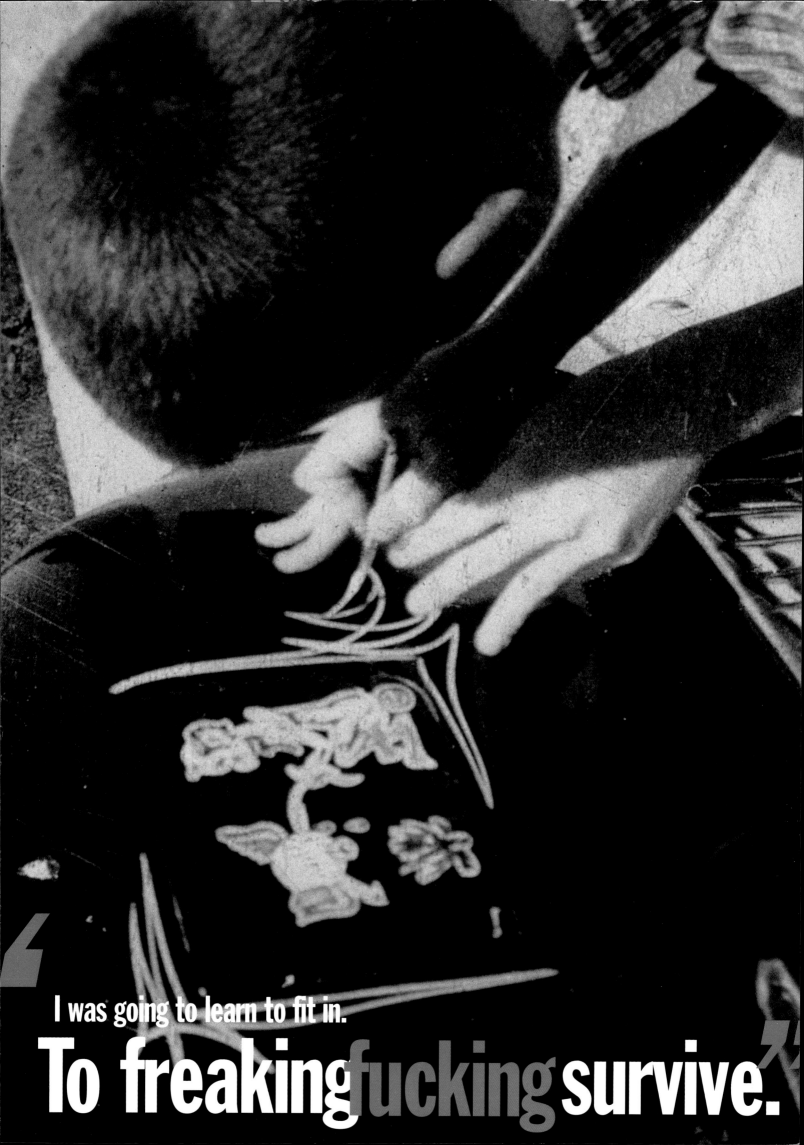

"I was going to learn to fit in.
To freaking fucking survive."

VISUALIZATION, PRESENTATION AND DRAFT EVASION

Chapter 4

My first legitimate design work in graphics came after the first year of college. I was home for the summer from The University of Southern California and my dad got me a job with a local architect.

I partied too much at night and kept falling asleep in the day on my drafting board. I was too sloppy and sleepy to do any drafting. It wasn't very interesting anyhow. One day, I took a pencil and redesigned the facade of a building that was being remodelled. Another day I redesigned the firm's card giving them a very Nike-like logo, which was pretty hip in the summer of the 'Twist'.

The happy and well-fed architect and his skinny son-in-law partner, looking like Sancho Panza and Don Quixote in reverse order, together congratulated me and made me, with no increase in pay of course, an official designer for The Firm. The experience of working for the happy windmill hunters served me well in my next life.

I left Michigan to go to school again in California. I made it as far as junior college in San Diego and another architecture firm that was also staying afloat with graphic design. I couldn't render their buildings without spilling paint all over the furniture so they let me sweep floors and learn graphic design production. I learned more. I quizzed them about type. I asked about illustration and photography and they taught me colors and design and design history.

At college I was writing, having my heart broken again — this time by a blonde cheerleader two classes ahead of me at a more important state university. And, I was catching up on the required subjects I needed for a degree. Subjects like algebra and draft dodging. The Vietnam War was starting to interfere with my surfing.

Like architecture, surfing has served me well. I fell in love with the culture when I saw my first 'woody' full of blonde girls in bikinis and blonde guys in baggy shorts, all topped with a full rack of surfboards. I talked my way into trading design for boards. I created the Gordon and Smith, Gotcha, MCD and Birdwell Beach Britches logos. All in use today. I can't walk into a beach parking lot without seeing some of my life's work. I learned all of the cool things about surfing and I learned how to make boards. I went to New York to be the first there to make boards and take orders for custom surf trunks.

I also designed the boss' logo — Hannon Surfboards. It was another swoosh-like beauty.

When I got to New York the sun came out like clockwork precisely on Memorial Day. Three months later at the end of summer, it got cold on cue. After Labor Day no one came to the beach. There would be no surfing customers until next summer. We closed the factory, and with two other guys I drove a much-in-demand, grey market VW Beetle back to California in three days non-stop. We sold it at a big profit and then I blew my share of that and my surfboard earnings on a car. So, broke, without a job and living in San Diego — a town full of sailors but no women, probably because it was full of sailors — I was away from all the action. I tried something new to get work. Self-promotion. Direct mail self-promotion.

I had gotten into trouble in high school for creating editorial cartoons that I somehow felt told the truth. The truth about sex, and the truth about the slavish ways in which teenagers succumbed to fad and fashion — my specialty. I got into trouble but I got

and talks
the talk"

'He walks
the walk

shopping to go Sure

shopping

to go Sure

Chapter

designing

cultural

revolution

5

What is Gotcha? Gotcha is a multi-million dollar international surfwear brand that traces its roots to a couple of guys printing t-shirts in a Laguna Beach garage. **How did you get that assignment?** Well, we have to back up a bit. I surf. And I have created logos, ads, clothing, fabric designs, packaging... for some of the majors in the surfing market – O'neill, O.P., Gordon and Smith, Body Glove. I was the first art director of 'Surfer Magazine'. When Gotcha found us I was trying to redesign 'Surfing Magazine'. I know surfing and I know the California youth market. Gotcha was a natural fit. **Mike Salisbury – Surf Marketing Guru?** Sort of. My redesign of 'Surfing Magazine' was the first attempt to appeal to the new global surfer. **Did it work?** Well, The new surfer was not just a Californian phenomenon, not only an American phenomenon – there were Australians, South Africans and South Americans surfing. This new world order of surfing was innovative and adventurous. They developed the short surfboard and radical moves. They chipped away the parochial facade of the sixties with new styles and attitudes, they were open-minded and unprejudiced. They even created a language of their own. The new look we created for 'Surfing Magazine' was a hit with the new surfer. 'Surfing''s circulation figures passed 'Surfer's' – the first magazine of surfing. But the majority of advertisers in the magazines were not appealing to the new surfers. **They were older, more provincial Californians for the most part and they were still using old-fashioned homemade ads weren't they?** Yes, but Gotcha wanted to give surfers ads of their own – ads for the MTV generation. So, they came to us. **How did you do that?** We wanted to break away completely from all the tired clichés of the old industry – blonde babes in bikinis with some guy who hadn't combed his hair in a week wearing shorts that were too tight. The first Gotcha ad ran across two pages – we kept a beautiful girl in the shot, but she was a brunette and in a one-piece bathing suit. The two surfer guys had their faces obscured in the billow of a parachute. **Not very Frankie and Annette.** That was the first. And a first in its own right. For every placement afterward we created a totally different ad. For every ad we created a new look. **No ad ever ran twice?** No. The message was always fresh. New. Different. If you missed it, too bad. **Would you consider it a**

campaign? Yes, why pay for expensive media when you have nothing to say? Don't buy time or space without a campaign. And a concept to fill it. But we put a unique spin on the idea of what a campaign is. Our premise: don't bore kids with repetition; they're not patient enough and will not tolerate it, nor do they have the attention span required to register the same message over and over. They get it the first time. We created a different ad for each exposure, to maximize the media investment. To keep them looking for the next one. Consistently inconsistent – very zen. **What about all those different Gotcha logos?** No two Gotcha logos looked exactly alike. We built a brand based on stimulating the market place with constant change. The brand became important as the symbol of change and the logo represents the brand. Ultimately the logo was the merchandise, the clothing just a vehicle for the brandmark. **Why do your ads look a lot like Calvin Klein and Esprit ads?** They look like ours. **Why?** It takes good clients to make good creatives. Gotcha was a good client – helpful, trusting and progressive. Together we were able to do a lot of pioneering in advertising graphics and styling. We were imitated – the ultimate compliment. **So where did all of this pioneering design and radical strategies get Gotcha?**

> *Only a few star designers have entered the ranks of celebrity, at least within the design world – Paul Rand, who put the ribbon on the UPS box; Milton Glaser, with his poster of Bob Dylan surrounded by a rainbow aura; and David Carson, who shook things up when he created a look for 'Ray Gun' magazine and let the type run wild over the page... Mike Salisbury is one of those people.*

Roger Black
formerly of 'Rolling Stone', 'New York Magazine', 'New West'

continued on page 26

I STARTED OUT

TRADING LOGO DESIGNS FOR SURFBOARDS... MONEY ITSELF IS NOT ALWAYS THE ANSWER.

THE SURFER

BI-MONTHLY
A John Severson Production

75¢

VOL. 3 NO. 3   AUG. – SEPT.

THE INTERNATIONAL SURFING MAGAZINE

MORE OF MURPHY

SURFING CHANGED MY

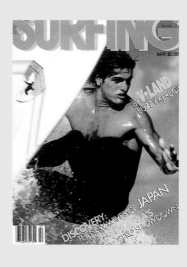

The Maui Pipeline Masters is renowned as being the pro surfing world's most balls-out event. This year, with the biggest swells from the unfavorable north, the surf never got perfect—but Pipe being Pipe, the surfers still faced more than their share of hideous oceanic drama....

by TIM BAKER

PIPE

Sunny Garcia takes a heavy wipeout during the Masters finals, torn arm muscles and all
PHOTO: Jeff Hornbaker

Surfing MAGAZINE

SURFER

"You always want some *glory* in your life."

Surfing MAGAZINE

HAWAII

NINETY-TWO

EXPLODES!

Laird Hamilton

continued from page 19

In 10 years, they were selling **$200,000,000** Gotcha's annually, retail. Gotcha became the number one brand in surfwear. They eventually crossed over into mainstream department stores and became more than surfwear – they became resortwear. Sportswear. More than a brand. **Why is Gotcha more than a brand?** We created a brand and a line of clothes based on designs of the brand name as the product – a new level of brand awareness. The Gotcha brand became shorthand for cool for a new breed of surfer. That shorthand translated to the mainstream and catapulted Gotcha to the top of the industry. Gotcha captured cool. We gave them the rope.

LWAYS WORKING ON THE EA, NOT THE LAST. THAT'S CRITI-CAL IN THIS BUSI-NESS."

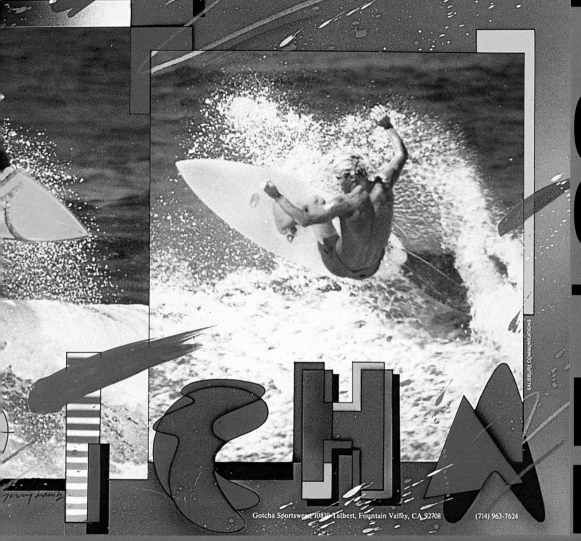

Gotcha Sportswear, 10810 Talbert, Fountain Valley, CA 92708   (714) 963-7624

MICHAEL TOMPSON
PRESIDENT, GOTCHA

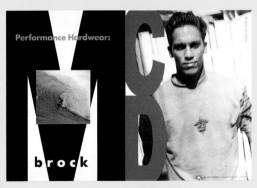

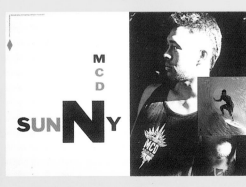

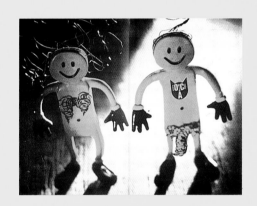

"When talking fashion, you gotta be where the customer isn't... in front. And when talking to young people, remember they are smart and fast. They get things the first time... don't repeat yourself."

Looking for a job I analysed what I could offer and where I wanted to go. I loved editorial work. I never had worked on anything but school publications and small magazines in San Diego, but I was a magazine fan. **I could draw and create cartoons with content.** I could design. So I created a mailer that would go to a potential employer that I felt could use my services. I also surfed and knew surfing. I created a cartoon mailer for the one place I really wanted to work — the brand new 'Surfer Magazine'. I wanted the mailer to get me attention like my high school cartoons did. It did.

I got the job. I was made the art director, ad designer, reporter, cartoonist and production person. The first day on the job I spilled rubber cement on the floor of the brand new offices, melting the entire linoleum-like surface of my work place.

The publisher promised to pay my way for an entire winter season of surfing in Hawaii when he took me on. He let me go right after I signed the lease for the very first place I ever had on my own. I couldn't pay the rent. I couldn't pay for my car. Was it the rubber cement incident?

No. I think I screwed up. I wanted to show off and I bragged to my boss about the owner of a newer surf magazine courting me to be his art director. After the sacking I went back to school. The Army was soon calling, but they couldn't get me if I was in college. For a while. **Before I left 'Surfer' I was sent on an errand.**

To Hollywood. Dick Dale was the hottest thing in music and another reason I had left San Diego.

Dick was The King of the 'Surf Guitar'. His song 'Miserlou' loudly opens 'Pulp Fiction'. That was the kind of energy that filled the Rendezvous Ballroom in Balboa, California, when he played. And I mean filled. Looking down from the balcony, nothing could be seen in the twinkling light reflected off the giant mirror ball in the ceiling but bouncing sun-bleached blonde hair. On boys and girls. It was wall-to-wall writhing and bobbing and weaving, and your ears would go numb with the sound of 4,000 bare feet stomping. 'The Surfer Stomp'. It was Dick Dale's theme and the biggest dancing mania to hit 'The Wonderbread' wonder of Southern California since the babies started booming. **Dick was The King of Surfing but he had a problem. He didn't surf.**

Dick came to John Severson, the publisher of 'Surfer', to make him look like a surfer at least in print. His first album of surf music was soon to be released, and he couldn't have a surf album without a picture of him surfing. This album job was to be for me two big lessons learned. Lesson One: if you creatively crop and tilt a picture you can design it to make anything or anyone look better. Years later as a creative director in the music business, I was to learn how effective this technique of 'The Dutch Angle' was when working with

I think I screwed

bad photos of rock stars. John took 'The King of Surfing' to a safe little beach and pushed him out to sea on a optimistically buoyant surfboard. **One can't really float on a board or ride one without some momentum.** The ocean was almost as flat as a plate that day. Safe for 'The King', but hard to surf on. So John pushed him out into the water and Dick did stand up for at least one shot.

The picture that came back from the lab was him. He was standing on a surfbaord. He was in a wave. It was barely ankle-high though, so Severson tilted the picture, cropped it judiciously, added some rubbery looking lettering of the title, and bingo — an actual surf music album with The King of the whole wet mess appearing on the cover as though he was actually surfing. Lesson Two: ask for the money. Severson had me deliver the album artwork to Dick at the Palladium Ballroom in far off Hollyweird. We practiced the hand-off before I left the beach-side offices of 'Surfer'. "Check goes into your hand first," barked John. "Then and only then does the art go into anyone else's hand."

He patted me on the back, handed me the package and wished me well on my mission to the big city. I was not any less shy than I ever was, but the fear of failure prevented me from shrinking from my duty. But as a back-up measure, I took along Rick Griffin, the magazine's real cartoonist, for support. Rick was like a big sheepdog, sweet and loyal but not a hard core grinder. **The two of us looking like The Beachboys' version of The Cowardly Lion and The Tin Woodsman set off for Oz.**

And the Palladium was lit up like The Emerald City. Inside, on a balcony a little too stained from years of spilled drinks and cigarette burns, I was introduced to Dick's father and manager. A little short guy, in a suit that couldn't be buttoned over his stomach, with a cigar butt clenched between his teeth. He stuck his hand out for the artwork. Silently. "John said you would have the money for the art". **Said I in my best imitation of bravery.** "Don't worry about the money, Severson said I could send him a check later". The sentence fell on the floor like another greasy spot. "No, I must have that check." said the boyscout in me. Mumble. Grumble. More little greasy blobs on the carpet. He waddled off, and then returned from the red velvet dungeon of the office buried in the wallpaper, with an envelope.

It was the check, I handed over the goods.
Mission accomplished. Lesson learned. When dealing with any client, money talks. And it should be the first to speak.

I couldn't pay the rent.

I couldn't pay for my car.
Was it the **rubber cement** *incident?*

6

JUMPING INTO THE WORLD OF MADISON AVENUE
YOU CAN SELL WITHOUT WORDS

I did my duty but got canned anyhow so I was back in school but still I needed a job. I picked the very best place to work at something I wanted to do and it was right in my neighborhood, right on the beach. It was an advertising agency and a very creative and innovative guy ran it. A guy that was so right so often hat no one could work for him. Phil Lansdale. I had so much respect for him, he was right. He was so right he got tired of telling clients how to get rich that he went into business for himself and soon got richer than those whiney clients who didn't appreciate him until he was gone.

Working for him at the beach meant I could have it all. I did try to get a job in L.A. about 30 miles north of Balboa but the working conditions were dreadful. I was introduced to a medieval concept straight from Monty Python — the bullpen. I didn't have to sit in a narrow closet with a bunch of other guys drawing type all day — I had ambition. I was going to be an art director in advertising and use someone else to draw the type. I drove back to the beach on my last dollar's worth of gas and I created a portfolio of ads that matched Phil's style. I got the job. So, I got married. I had to; the Army was taking college students that were single.

At Phil's I learned that people will read long copy in ads, but you need to get their attention first: Phil liked to use great art to stop the reader. I learned that you could communicate without words if you use ideas and I learned the value of merchandising. Phil knew how to get stuff sold, in ads and at point-of-sale. We had a shoe store chain as a client and Phil insisted that all of he handbags be left all over the floor so they would be the cause of a little impulse buying by the lady customers. He only advertised to men on Saturdays in the morning paper on a right-hand page in the main news section. He started 4-Day Tire Stores and 4-day Golf Stores because he felt men only shopped on four days of the week. He offered selection and discount pricing on quality brands. To see what actually happened at the retail level with the actual customers, store checks were the norm for him. It all worked. It still does.

true.

Neutrogena

A Vectra? No, this is much cool. A Mondeo? No, come off it. This one's much more fun. What is it?

THE NEW S5 FROM THE NEW SEAT

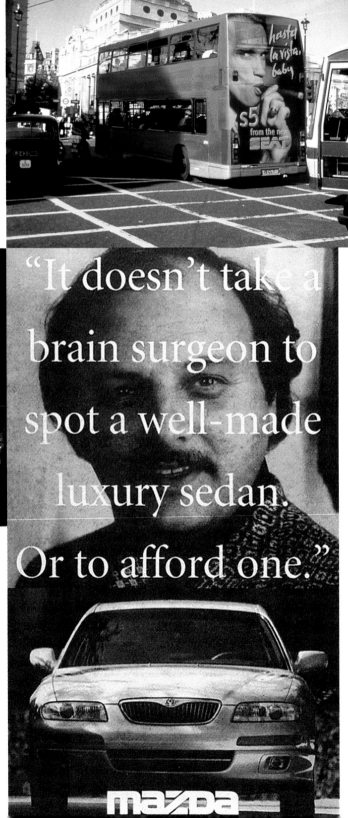

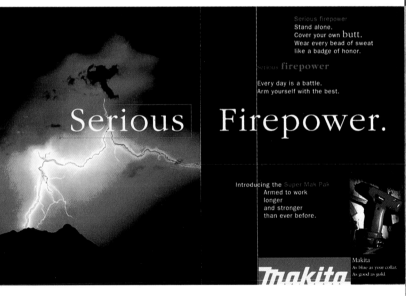

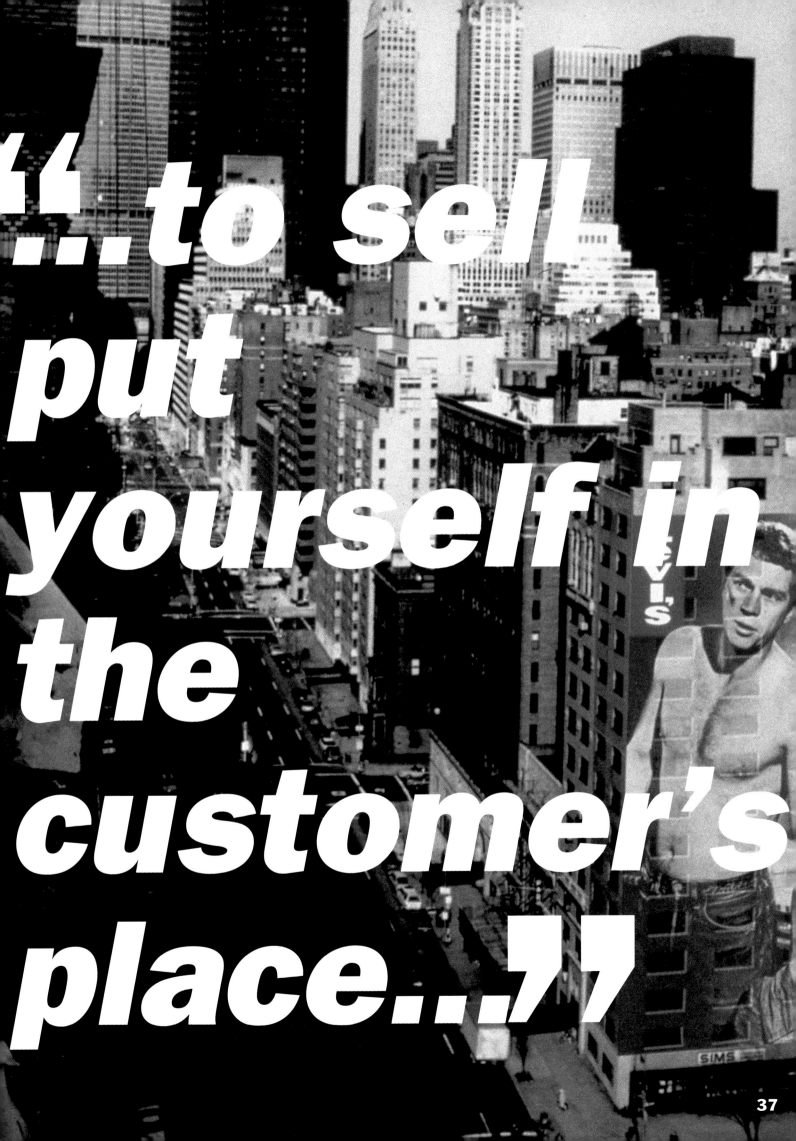

"...to sell put yourself in the customer's place..."

ba
off road

Baja

"Mike's work

is

where
the
pavement
stops

As Baja's most well-respected and successful off road tour operator, Baja Off Road Tours has over eight years experience in taking both the seasoned off road rider as well as the novice on safe, memorable trips. Baja Off Road Tours is endorsed by the Governor of Baja California, the Secretary of Tourism for Baja California, and the Policia Federal De Caminos, or Federal Highway Patrol. There is no other off road tour operator in Baja, or Mexico for that matter, with the credentials and experience of Baja Off Road Tours. Baja Off Road Tours is recognized as the leader by Team Green, Kawasaki's amateur racing department and by Kawasaki Motors Corp., U.S.A.

Baja Off Road Tours has been featured in Men's Jo Cycle News, Cycle Worl Dirt Rider and Kawasaki's Team Green News and has been televised on ESPN, ESPN2, EXTRA!, Motoworld and Motoworld 2. In addition to all this enthusiastic coverage Baja Off Road Tours has also been featured in European and Japanese magazines.

BAJA
of
road
tours
begin

you

are here

cinemagraphic

he tells stories.
You don't have to be art aware to get it."

Robert Pelton
designer, author
'The World's Most Dangerous Places'

BLOWN

AWAY

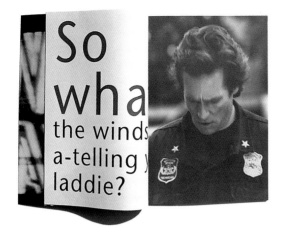

So wha the winds a-telling y laddie?

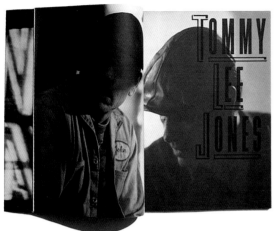

TOMMY LEE JONES

1:21:09:21.1 115I00044+02
1:25:48:17.2 115I00462+07
1:30:19.2 114I00185+0

I do it my way and the client's

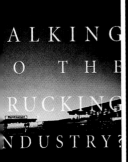

ALKING O THE RUCKING NDUSTRY?

...NEWPORT IS MOVING RIGHT ALONG WITH THIS HIGH VELOCITY BUSINESS TRAFFIC IN...

354 six maximum performance MEDIA VEHICLE

NEWPORT
COMMUNICATIONS

"I wish they all could

Now don't tell me you designed Robert Redford? No, we designed the team logo and uniforms for his movie 'The Natural'. **Why does the logo look so primitive?** We went way back to the very early days of baseball to get the proper look. I prefer to call it authentic. **Is authenticity important?** It is if you want to make something believable. People today have incredibly high visual standards. **Why is this logo in here... in this book?** I have created logos for corporations and stores and films and products... but this was our first for a team. **Was this a brand?** Yes, though not a traditional branding project, the uniform and logo needed to capture the essence of an era – to communicate the right message in a manner appropriate to the product. In a word – branding.

be California Girls."

PHOTOGRAPHED BY

clive mcclean

Photographed by
onathan   Lenna

"girls

I chose to be ambitious. I armed myself for opportunity. I went back to school. I had learned a lot at the small college I was attending before I got the job with Lansdale. I finally got art history because it was taught visually like it should be. I learned more about writing and I killed in graphic design. I just didn't have any challenges. I needed to take classes from professionals. That could only be done in Los Angeles.

Every evening after work I would drive up to L.A. from the beach to attend ad design classes at Chouinard — a school specializing in fine and applied art.

At the agency I was coming up with concepts, designing ads, illustrating and doing all of the production art. With this schedule, finishing homework on time was not easy. My one excuse for not having the assignment completed for class was my last. I didn't have the time. I meekly told the teacher — a nice mild mannered man by the name of Marv Rubin.

He lost his sweet smile, narrowed his eyes, bent towards me and growled in a fashion not unlike Jack Webb in 'Dragnet'. "Make the time."

After that I made the time. And I made my work better than anybody elses. That work got me hired by 'Playboy'. A big time job. A real company in a real city — Chicago. I was stoked. My wife wasn't. It wasn't the nature of the magazine that disturbed her, she just did not want to leave home. I convinced her to go for my resume. And our future.

She went to Chicago but her folded arms never left the tight placement they were held in right under the permanent scowl on her lips. This was not the first time my ambition got in the way of a relationship.

The big surprise at 'Playboy' was that nobody was in a hurry. Things were so slow people would go to the movies all day and never be missed. My boss was always behind the locked doors of his office with his secretary. So I learned.

'Playboy' is the model every other skin magazine desires to be. Like 'Rolling Stone' later would be when I helped redesign it, 'Playboy' was an overwhelmingly successful packaging of outlaw content. Both put acceptable clothing on sex, drugs and rock and roll. 'Playboy' had the best pacing, the best printing, the best photography, art and design in its category. It was better looking and more carefully executed than most magazines. They even had editors who proofread the copy — words set in real metal — just for rivers and widows. I learned all I could. I asked all the questions I could think of and I learned. I learned not only all I could learn about editorial design, I learned about writing and art and the designers responsibility to make things read. The words came first at 'Playboy'. I remember the editor walking past my office with a paste-up in his hand of the lead article for an upcoming issue grumbling, "Dumb frigging art directors can't read."

I picked that mechanical up off the floor where he had thrown it and saw what he meant. The type, an entire page of it, was all set in nine point Baskerville, a small typeface but effective enough to lend class to the page when used in narrow columns with normal punctuation. Here was an entire page width of grey without even paragraphs — just little p symbols. He was right. You could not read it.

I never wanted to be called a dumb frigging art director. I have respect for the message. If they can't read it, they won't buy it. And the job of any person who creates for commerce whether it be in editorial design, graphic design, advertising, movie making, games or music is to have the stuff we communicate with communicate. Even if it communicates in a code of typographic abstraction like some design targeted to younger niche groups does, it still must communicate something or the work will die an unnoticed death at the point-of-sale if it gets there at all. We art directors and designers are all salespeople selling visually with magazine design and packaging and logos and ads and menus and brochures, signs, websites and TV.

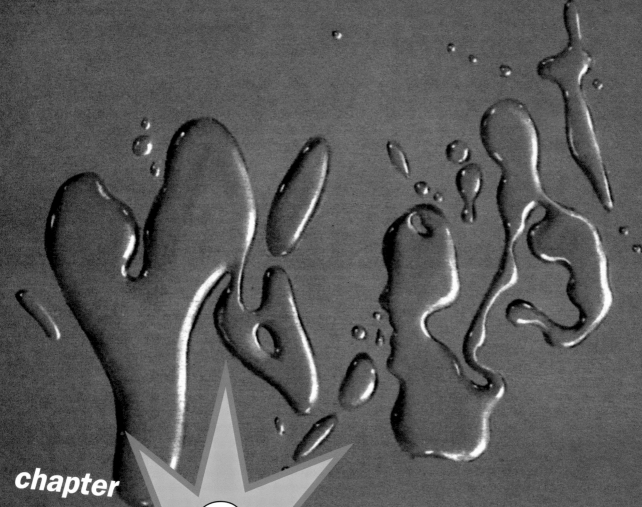

chapter

8

WEST MAGAZINE

BRINGING THE CALIFORNIA THING TO THE WORLD

I didn't even know what I was going to do, I just knew I would learn a lot and get noticed.

I left 'Playboy' to go somewhere that had a faster pace to suit my Attention Deficit Disorder and to try and get a smile on my wife's face. I got a job the same way as I got the 'Surfer' job. I chose to be ambitious. I chose the place I wanted to work in a location that my wife wanted to live. Advertising was where I wanted to be. I wanted to be creating modern advertising for print and TV. California is where she wanted to be.

I targeted my potential employer with something creative that would show them what I had to offer. I did not have a great portfolio full of ads. **But I could solve problems creatively.** I had a problem — getting a job. How did I solve that problem? I think of myself as a client. What was my client's **Unique Selling Proposition?** Attention-getting communication. How did I sell that before? I mailed a cartoon strip of my life story to Carson-Roberts, the most creative agency in L.A. At Carson-Roberts I created, directed, illustrated and edited my first TV commercial and won my first major international award for broadcast. **I had just turned 23. Already I was bored.**

The 'Los Angeles Times West Magazine' — a large format Sunday supplement was one year old. It looked like crap. Jim Bellows would go on to great things in TV creating the first weekly entertainment news programming, but at this time he was an editor at 'The Times' and he was looking to make his baby of a magazine work and look better. Larry Dietz was a writer for 'West' and his roommate was the TV journalist Joel Siegle. At this time in history, Joel, along with artist Ed Ruscha, director Terry Gilliam and myself were all working at Carson-Roberts. Larry told Joel that Bellows was looking for an art director, Joel told me and against everyone's good advice I took the job. It made me famous, **I won every award I ever wanted to win**, I taught myself photography and took pictures for every magazine I had ever wanted to take pictures for. I was getting high on the attention I was getting.

It was a great feeling of accomplishment because I started that job without a clue. I didn't know how to be the number one art director on a magazine. But, I knew I had a huge captive audience to promote myself to and a bigger audience with the international mailing list I created. I knew that this magazine looked so bad that anything I did would only make it look better.

It was large and it was on newsprint. Newsprint is so forgiving — anything looks great on it because no one expects anything to look good on it. My first task was to take something I learned from 'Playboy' and adapt good pacing to 'West'. We only had a few pages — why ruin the illusion of this being a real magazine by starting articles on half pages or right-hand pages? I commissioned good art just like 'Playboy' would. I then established a format grid and typography system to give a consistent look to the magazine until I got more confident with my design. To get attention I began creating covers that were ideas. **Visual metaphors** — a photograph of a wedge of Swiss cheese with a candle stuck in it over a caption that read Happy Birthday Mickey Mouse. Photo of a taco stand with a sign that said Home of Kosher Burritos. These were all puns just like my high school cartoons were only they didn't get me in trouble, **they just got the magazine and me attention and me a beautiful, new future ex-wife.**

When I got bored with all of that I produced articles on the California thing. I was a product of this environment. **I loved it.** And a lot of it was disappearing under the growing destruction of the population vomit that was covering my home. I wasn't hired to do anything but art direct this throwaway and I wound up having it be my vehicle. How? I felt that a magazine from Southern California — the popular culture fountainhead of the world — should reflect what it was.

I had great support from Marshall Lumsden the editor and Bellows who acted as our publisher. I overcame my shyness, the fear of possible rejection I had learned from the constant negative response to me from my parents and **I just took a deep breath and asked for the extra assignments.** I made a presentation of my ideas and I sold them. But my concepts and wants were not entirely self-serving. I was also thinking in terms of what the others I was working with wanted. I treated them like clients. Bellows wanted a magazine that would position us to advertisers as the voice of California. I think Marshall just liked the idea of me doing a lot of the work.

Cover 1
LOS ANGELES TIMES JANUARY 4, 1970

west

The Chinatown Revolution
Yellow Power And The Old Way

Cover 2
LOS ANGELES TIMES MARCH 29, 1970

west

HOLLYWOOD AND THE MOON

Cover 3
LOS ANGELES TIMES AUGUST

west

'DON'T SWAT! WE'RE YOUR FRIENDS'
(Such are the dreams of the everyday housefly . . .)

Cover 4
LOS ANGELES TIMES JANUARY 30, 19

west

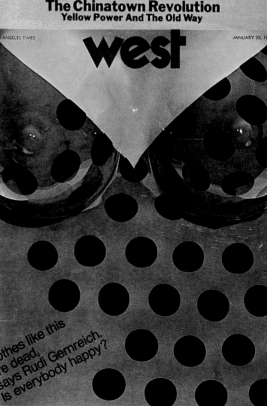

othes like this
re dead,
says Rudi Gernreich.
Is everybody happy?

Cover 5
LOS ANGELES TIMES APRIL 30, 1972

west

**One Day
in the Life of
A20284**

Cover 6
LOS ANGELES TIMES

west

RECYCL
LOS ANGE

Q&A: FRED HAR
THE OUTSPC

OF UNION

Cover 7
LOS ANGELES TIMES APRIL 25, 197

west

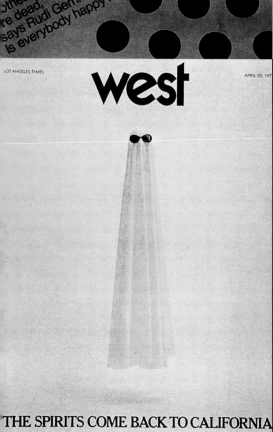

THE SPIRITS COME BACK TO CALIFORNIA

Cover 8
LOS ANGELES TIMES OCTOBER 13, 1968

west

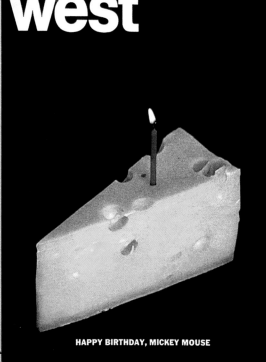

HAPPY BIRTHDAY, MICKEY MOUSE

Cover 9

west

Preserving San Francisco

LOS ANGELES TIMES FEBRUARY 7, 1971

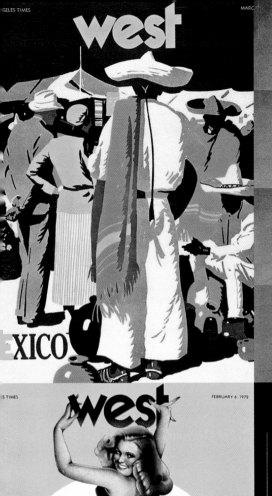

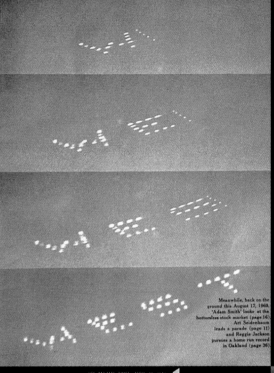

EXICO

SOLAR POWER
Let the Sunshine Do It

A NOSTALGIC LOOK AT THE ART OF NEON

L.A.'S RECORDING GAME ON A PLATTER

OCTOBER 11, 1970

SLOW SCHOOL ZONE

Goodbye, Ed Sullivan

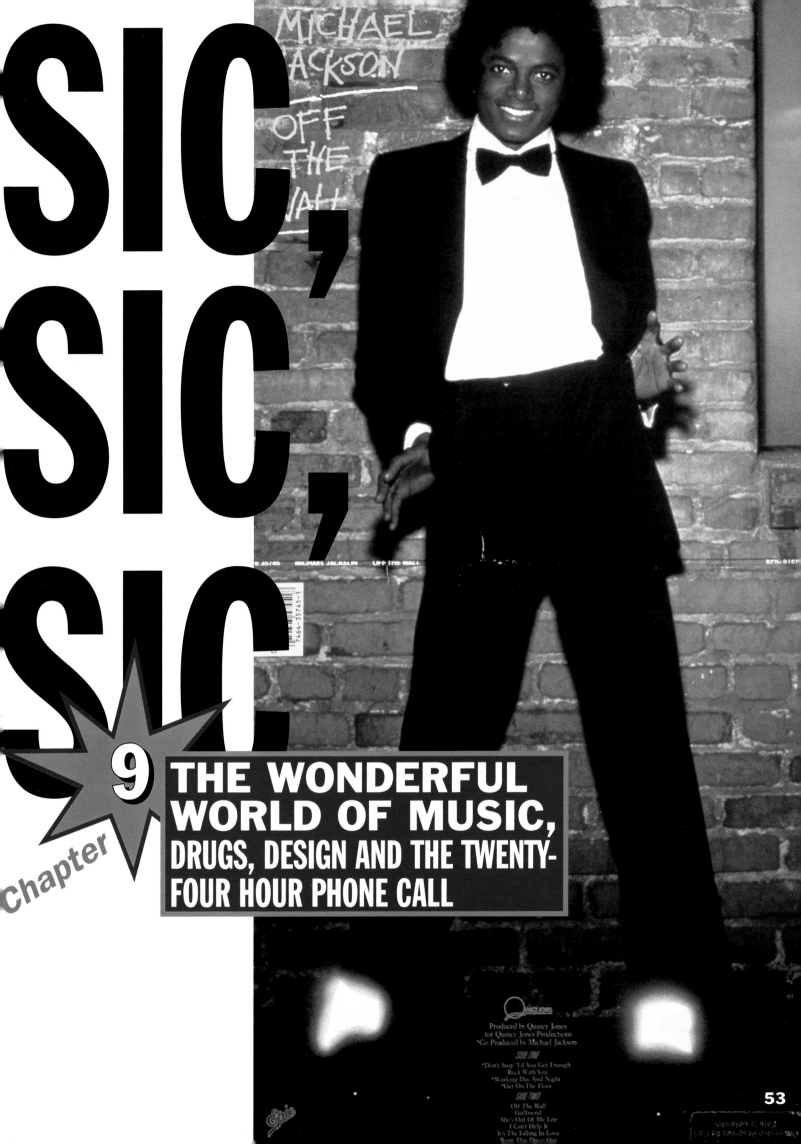

SIC, SIC, SIC,

Chapter 9

THE WONDERFUL WORLD OF MUSIC, DRUGS, DESIGN AND THE TWENTY-FOUR HOUR PHONE CALL

53

How do you design a person? I was knocked out by Michael Jackson's performance in 'The Wiz'. My instincts told me this kid would be HUGE. His manager at the time had worked with me at UA Records. He called one day and told me Michael was going solo, and he needed help. Picture this... for Michael Jackson's first album – 'Off the Wall' – they had him sitting on a hay bale wearing an outfit from Hee Haw. It's true – the initial "concept" for the first album was as lame as that. **What were you there for?** I was there for what may have been a first in the recording business. I designed a person and created a brand identity for him. **Not just a cover?** No. **How?** An entire look was created that would present him as a star. He was made a visual metaphor for success. **A brand icon.** Yes. And Michael Jackson was in the shadows in the room when I presented my design for him. **Did he say anything?** Only when I finished my pitch, he simply said softly "Thank you very much". That's it. **End of story?** Weeks later I was called back to the

On the effect of 'New West' on Los Angeles culture: "We fanned the flame of absurdity and dada. Melrose before West was like SoHo. Who was there? Photographers, artists, lofts. It was kind of serious. Then suddenly it turned. You had nostalgia, Hawaiian shirts for sale. Total absurdity as fashion.

Roland Young
Art Center College of Design,

agent's office. He wasn't smiling. Michael was there too but not in the shadows this time... and he looked very stern. This did not look or feel good to me. No one spoke. I wasn't even offered coffee. Not even old coffee. Long pregnant pause... "He likes the idea" the agent mumbled. "Just add white socks" chimed Michael. **How about the glove?** My concept was bought. A slightly built shy boy had just been packaged for his solo debut – in a tux – combining two symbols to create a visual metaphor for bigtime talent with glittery white sox and one white glove. **End of story?** That was the easy part. Getting the tux was hard. We finally found an Yves St. Laurent ladies tux. **Ladies tux?** We're not talking Arnold here. **The glove?** Bob Mackey. He made the sox and glove with lots of glitter and glitz. Yves and Mackey. **Then what?** We shot all around L.A. – Michael even changed in the ladies room of the Planeterium. But nothing clicked. There was no magic. **Just a young kid in a tux?** Tux and glove and white sox... but the sox weren't working. **How did you make it work – tux and white sox?** I flashed back to Fred Astaire and Gene Kelly and Cary Grant. They made fashion history with white sox. They put their hands in the pockets of their slacks to pull the pants high enough to show the sox. "Michael, put your hands in your pockets. Thumbs out and pull your pants up. Flash! Flash! Flash! Flash! **The rest is pop history.**

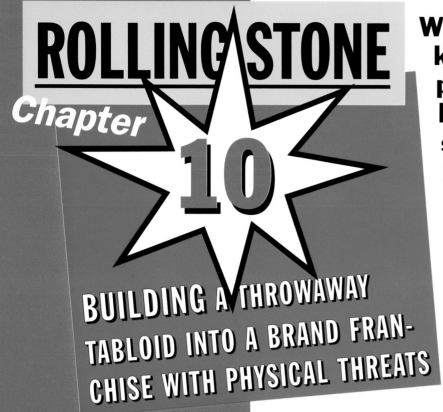

ROLLING STONE

Chapter

10

BUILDING A THROWAWAY TABLOID INTO A BRAND FRANCHISE WITH PHYSICAL THREATS

What is the most well known of all the publications that you have designed? 'Rolling Stone'. **What was your most challenging publication design assignment?** 'Rolling Stone'. **Wasn't 'Rolling Stone' already a successful magazine?** It was a newspaper. A tabloid. **How did you get the attention of 'Rolling Stone'?** We had designed or redesigned several magazines... winning more awards than any other art director... **More than any? Mike Salisbury?** Well, more than any art director in the West... ever. I take pictures for magazines – 'Esquire', 'Harper's', 'Vogue', 'Time', 'Look', 'Forbes' and 'Men's Journal'... my photos are in the permanent collection of the Museum of Modern Art. **But why did Rolling Stone really want you?** I had designed a Sunday supplement to a newspaper to look like a magazine. **But you never made a newpaper itself – as 'Rolling Stone' was – look like a magazine.** No. **This would be a challenge.** Yes and No. 'Rolling Stone', like most newspapers, had one typeface for subheads, one for bylines, and one for text. They were all the same typeface too. That was the easy part. Add typefaces. **The hard part?** The covers and the pacing. **Had they ever used anything on the**

cover except a picture of a rock and roll person? No. In fact, I was asked by Jann Wenner, the publisher, to create high-concept covers – which is my forte. Didn't it fold down the middle to a size about slightly larger than a TV guide? All in black and white on cheap newsprint. **That look really wasn't a problem to read, so why redesign?** It turned off advertisers. Not the music advertisers... but there were only so many of them. **'Rolling Stone' had the writing and editing to be big time didn't it?** It needed to look big time. **Why didn't every page in the magazine have that obituary rule box surrounding it?** Very San Francisco. Very Quasi-Victorian. **So how did you make 'Rolling Stone' into a magazine?** For me, photos make a magazine as well as words. Art makes a magazine. Pacing makes a better magazine. To pace 'Rolling Stone' I gave them spreads. Spreads of photos. Spreads of art. **Didn't 'Rolling Stone' have tons of word pages?** To be a magazine some of those words had to be cut, some of those oxford rule corrals had to be dumped and I had pictures run across two whole pages, in color, with headlines designed to compliment the picture, the illustration, or the story itself. **A magazine?** A magazine is a composition. Like music. That's pacing. We gave 'Rolling Stone' pacing. Big pictures. Small pictures. Prelude. Crescendo. Headlines. Initials. Captions. Strings. Brass. Percussion. Words and Music. 'Rolling Stone'. A Magazine.

At 'Rolling Stone', he was the first art director to bring a big-time sensibility. The previous art director had been the publisher's brother-in-law, a sculptor. He was very good, but Salisbury came in and ran incredible stuff. The publication came alive.

Steven Heller
Art Director, 'New York Times'

a magazine is a compos

To make it sing I gave

"Like Music...

big pictures."

Rolling Stone'

LOVE POLLUTION

Number Nine

Vietnam Rose is in town and she's looking for you. Rose, a strain of Super Clap, came back with our boys from Vietnam. What happened that many five-piaster ladies in the Nam contracted gonorrhea and tried to scrimp on the price of a doctor by using Black Market penicillin. Unfortunately, the illegal stuff was weak. The symptoms would dwindle while the malady lingered on, growing ever stronger, as VD will. Naturally, the girls our boys dated back home got Rose too, and when they turned themselves in to their doctors or clinics, they were hooted at and ridiculed to the point that—according to the Center for Disease Control in Atlanta (the most respected medical research agency in America)—many refused further treatment. So Vietnam Rose grew stronger. Worse, in their ignorance, stateside medics prescribed ordinary dosages of penicillin for a disease so potent it scarfed up antibiotics like chocolate mousse. It now takes five million units of penicillin

DEATH
and the
Surgeon

BY RICHARD SELZER

BLOOD, SWEAT
AND TEARS

eye tattooed
America

BALD CO

eteve Stills, Paul Simon, Neil Sedaka, Joe Cocker, Elton John and Mike Love are among the millions of Americans with a hair problem. Is there a solution for them? Yes. Dozens. Turn the page.

walk hard   walk tough

BY DAVID LILLARD
photography
courtesy of
JANSPORT

Sorting through the dozens of workout theories and techniques practiced in Southern California may be so difficult you'll want to throw in the towel. That's it!

This dynamic and unique stretch and strength workout uses a towel as a means of resistance to promote greater flexibility and muscular endurance. Body Lines combines music, body awareness, breathing techniques and exercise not only for increased strength, stretch and flexibility, but also for relaxation and stress reduction.

Many people practice both cardiovascular and strength training in a workout program, but neglect the stretching aspect of total fitness. There are many benefits to stretching other than increased range of motion and relaxation. Stretching often decreases the amount of muscular soreness and tension. By enhancing one's mobility, coordination skills are freer and easier. It promotes circulation and fosters a good feeling both physically and mentally. Through daily fitness and sports activities, muscles tighten and need to be stretched. Conversely, muscles overstretched by those repeated activities need to be strengthened.

Keeping strong abdominal support in mind, emphasis is placed on visualization, angle or arc produced towel, body and it Particular attention is proper alignment, b throughout all the mo and actually "feeling" geted muscle group th exercise addresses.

As a resistance tool, used in several ways to strength. As a stretci implement, it can be between the hands, roll small cylinder and se between the knees, pressed against while it floor.

As a stretching aid, can often serve us that a yourself. It can be around the foot to seated or lying humstring or held behind the back chest stretch. The tow visualization of a line, a limbs to parallel, exten angles around the t times, the towel can be participant with th padding needed for th hips and back or for when lying.

The strength exercise

Flex
time

by Valentin Swegle, m.s.   photographed by Greg Gorman
and Lennette Newell

Lines can increase the ability to sustain the po certain posture throu period of time. Various and isotonic strength m and static stretch techni used simultaneously in anced workout. Is contractions do not ch

Not that many Americans have the extraordinary visual brilliance of Mike. He can make visual statements that stop you cold. Practically every cover made you stop in a way that magazine covers no longer do. Mike would get [the painter] Ed Ruscha, and Ruscha would do a logo in water, because there was an article in 'West' that week on water, but you'd say, 'My God... Mike has more pure ideas than anyone I've ever come across.' Over a week, he could come up with 70 ideas for editorial stuff.

"Mike created "a remarkable sense of discovery, description and celebration of place. Once Mike pointed out a series of pictures and text blocks and said to me 'What if we did this with hamburgers?' So we did. I ate and measured hamburgers. 8 of them. It was just a spread. 'The Burger that Ate L.A.' One was so obviously the best – Cassell's, the 'Best Burger in L.A.' It appeared on Labor Day Sunday. On Monday, I went by to give the guy a paper in case he hadn't seen it, and the line was around the block, and it stayed around the block for months.

Larry Dietz, writer

Headlines.

Initials.

Captions.

Brass.

Strings.

Percussion.

"Words and music...

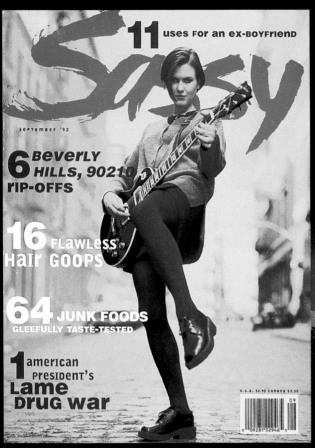

11 uses for an ex-BOYFRIEND

Sassy

september '92

6 BEVERLY
HILLS, 90210
RIP-OFFS

16 FLAWLESS
HAIR GOOPS

64 JUNK FOODS
GLEEFULLY TASTE-TESTED

1 american
PRESIDENT's
LAME
DRUG WAR

U.S.A. $2.95 Canada $2.50

WHEEL & RIM SPEC'ING • 'SLICK' RIG CONTROL
DRIVER MANAGEMENT • BRAINY BED BUGGING • BIG BRAKE STRUGGLE

OCTOBER 1996

Heavy Duty Trucking

The Business Magazine of Trucking

THE MARKET:
WHAT'S HOT, WHAT'S NOT

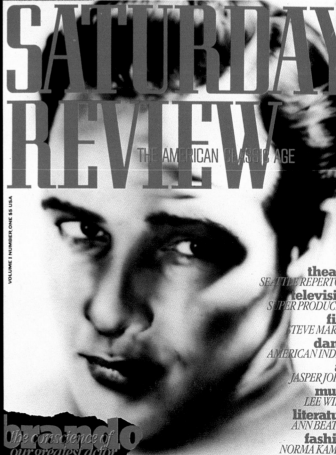

california
active
THE GUIDE FOR HEALTH, SPORTS & FITNESS

executive fitness
active fashion
earth day

spring
tune-up

california
calendar

🟠 EVENTS 🟠 RACES 🟠 CLUBS

SATURDAY
REVIEW
THE AMERICAN CLASSIC AGE

VOLUME I NUMBER ONE $5 USA

thea
SEATTLE REPERTO
televisi
SUPER PRODUC
fi
STEVE MAR
dan
AMERICAN IND
i
JASPER JO
mu
LEE WI
litera
ANN BEAT
fashi
NORMA KAM

brando
the conscience of
our greatest actor

...that's
pacing."

BONUS PAGES!

"Covers,
matchboo
same job
need th
type of
des

Do it with the Light on.

The Electric Light Orchestra
Fall Tour 1973

insider
CBS Affiliate Promotion
Fall 1997
Focus, Prioritize and Maximize

AUGUST 1997
VOLUME 10
ISSUE 4

Los Angeles International Film Exposition 1974   THE PARAMOUNT THEATRE IN HOLLYWOOD

CALIFORNIA
MOVIE

Capture America.

NEW AMERICAN WRITING

RICKIE LEE JONES

osters,

s do the

hey all

same

fficient

n."

TIME
FIFTY CENTS
COLONEL KURTZ
KURTZ
JULY 19, 1968

IN CONCERT
IN CONCERT
ELO

MAS

INTO THE PURPLE VALLEY
RY COODER

THE KNOCKOUT CC
AL
H
MAJO

"...nobody is convinced by the subjective: always tell a story."...

"All I could see were those little white globes that were Flynt's butt cheeks as he pumped some onlooker's wife... I was just there waiting to get my layouts approved."

After 'West' folded I had more job offers than I could handle. I tried a lot of them. I was creative director for United Artists Records where I saw the biggest pile of cocaine I had ever seen. I was in the fur-covered acid-green playroom of a famous R&B musician. On top of an orange laminated coffee table top in a silver sugar bowl were about two pounds of the stuff. I wasn't offered any. I didn't ask for any.

Two old friends from advertising asked me to join them as a partner in their new agency. I did and wound up on the boards all by myself while they ran around with babes in Porsches we couldn't afford.

I was hired by Frances Coppola to design his 'City Magazine' and wound up working on 'Apocalypse Now' and 'The Black Stallion' as a production designer. And George Lucas asked me to design 'The Art of Stars Wars' book and to create a logo for Industrial Light and Magic – his special effects unit. I was hired as a creative director at the Wells Rich Green and Foote Cone Belding ad agencies. Ricky Lee Jones kept me on the phone for about 8 hours and James Taylor, Ry Cooder, Randy Newman and George Harrison assigned me to create their album covers. My photography got into the Museum of Modern Art in New York and my design and advertising was placed in The Smithsonian and The Library of Congress. I taught at Art Center and U.C.L.A. and redesigned 'The San Francisco Examiner'.

Hefner had me back in Chicago to design the American edition of the French men's magazine 'Oui'. The editorial group from that venture went to L.A. to create a tasty, slick magazine to make a pornographer look good. That pornographer was Larry Flynt. Another attention-getting troublemaker who made me look like a lightweight.

The tight little group of editors never let me in to the girlie shoots but I did get to hear Larry tell about sex with chickens and I learned how they make a vagina look like candy. And with writer Terry Abrahamson I created the ad parody that got Flynt into the Supreme Court and onto the silver screen. I was a witness to most of that story. I was at his wedding and I was there at the 'Hustler' offices when he got shot. I didn't make it to Althea's funeral but I did help her with her punk magazine before she died of AIDS and I helped him with marketing and design for another attempt at a classy skin magazine.

'Rage' was meant to be not-your-father's 'Playboy'. It could have been a big success with the newer class of better informed horny young man, but Flynt was too impatient to wait for advertising dollars to hook in. He went the way that he always went to get the cash flowing for the gash – he went pink. Not just Flamingo-colored female genitalia, he had some magenta male members showing too. It was all too explicit. The newsstands dumped him and he dumped 'Rage'.

12

5

1

Creating the most well-known clothing brand in the world.

You say that you created that 'All American' icon Levi's 501? Yes. Levi's 501. **How?** For years, women in California had been remaking Levi's jeans for men by soaking them in warm bathtubs to shrink them to fit female bodies. Levi Strauss realized this and developed 'Levi's Shrink-to-Fit-Button-Fly-Jeans-for-Women.' My task was to create an advertising campaign to introduce this new, yet old product. **Why?** Research said that what was taken for

THE BIGGEST

granted in California – that you had to buy Levi's oversized and shrink them to fit – was largely unknown outside the West. My concept to present this new version of an American classic was to create a new symbol of communication to simply explain that what fits men now fits women. **How?** By using two easily understood and known symbols. A visual metaphor for this new product was created. I put a female in a well-known male situation: a situation in which jeans were an organic part of that situation. **What were those two symbols you combined?** The ultimate jeans' symbol to me was James Dean putting his feet up on the back of that

NUMBER

car seat, leaning back in the rear seat, slumped down with his hat pulled over his eyes. **'Giant'** Yes. My James Dean was a lady. **The other symbol.** Yes, a lady in men's jeans; the short version. **But how did you tell people**

all the details behind getting these Levi's to fit their behinds? For that, long copy print ads with well-defined illustrations outlining the whole shrink system were created. A step-by-step how to do it. **But where's the 501 part?** Originally the tagline to accompany the ad was 'Levi's Shrink-to-Fit-Button-Fly-Jeans-Now-Cut-For-Women'. That's kind of a lot of words for the teeny little space left over on a billboard, print ad or TV screen. **Who**

LITTLE

needs words? The client needs words... that's who. It's their product. But we needed a catch – no one would remember to say all of that when they went in to ask for some jeans. We needed a brand. "Just call the damn things what we all call them. 501s" – the internal stocking number – "and trademark it!"... I said. **That's it? That's how Levi's 501 came to be the most well-known brand of clothing in history?** It was a combination of everything – simplifying a wordy tagline to a number and reinforcing it with a cohesive, strategic ad campaign. **Thus the most**

IN CLOTHING

famous clothing brand in the world was given to the public to use 100 years after it's invention: Levi's 501 jeans.

"The trick in getting a client is to have that doesn't look li

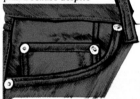

"Usually it's
the obvious

76

BIG FAT RED TAB

that escapes people, like the world's most famous jeans not even having a brand name, or the fact that Joe Camel was already on the packet."

Levi's Tab

bikers

surfers

artists

poets

stars

black, blue and cool

art guy

Power

levis Guys

"FOR ME,

Name that dude contest

the outsiders 1985

MAIL TO SAN FRANCISCO
LEVIS 43748

NAME

ADDRESS

WHERE DO YOU SHOP?

there's no better advertising medium than a well designed magazine dedicated to a product, place or service."

79

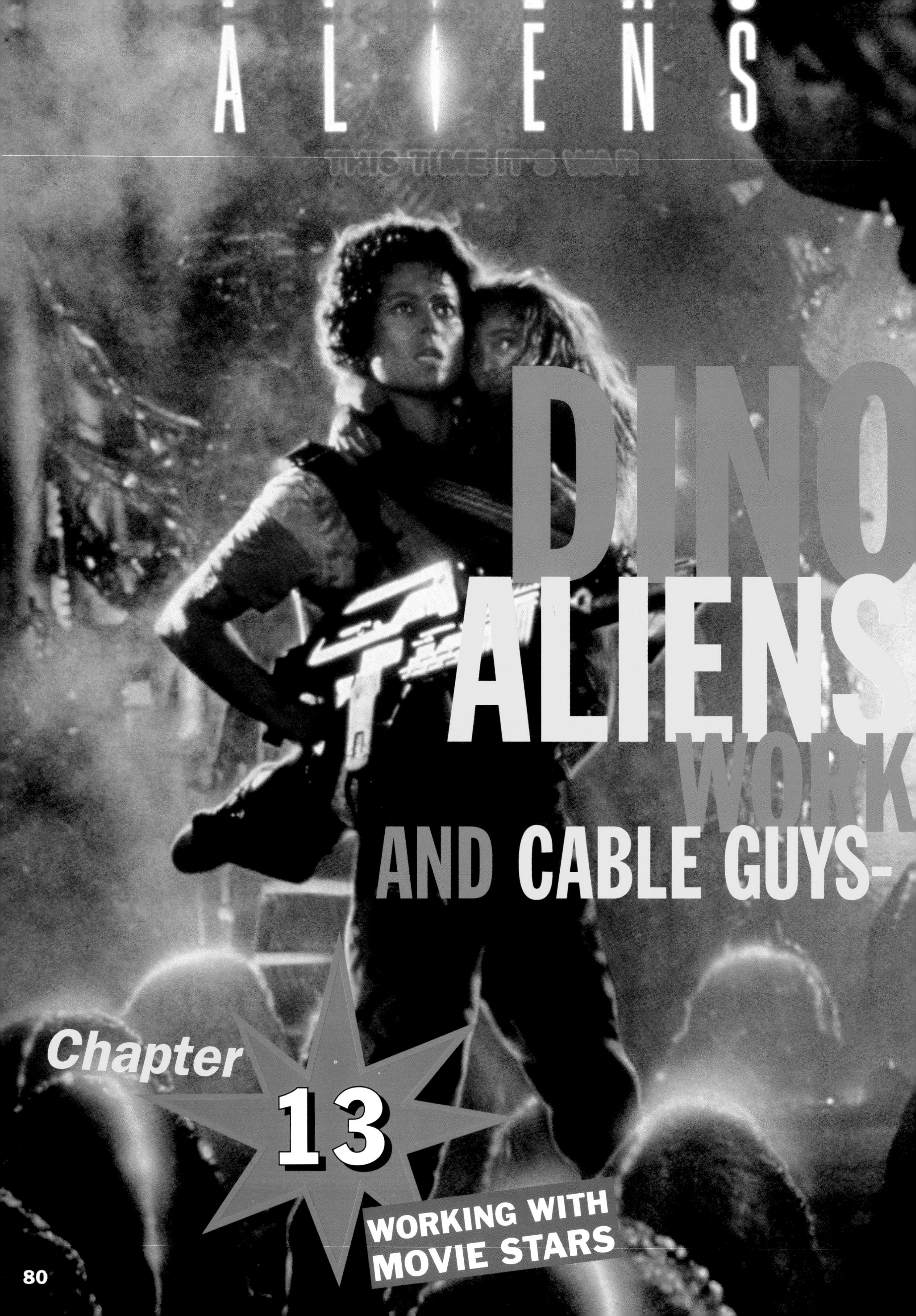

ALIENS

THIS TIME IT'S WAR

DINO ALIENS WORK AND CABLE GUYS—

Chapter

13

WORKING WITH MOVIE STARS

How do you follow one of the world's all-time great motion picture advertising images of that creepy 'ALIEN' egg? I didn't. The live talent in 'ALIEN' was unknown. The star of the original movie was the alien. So the sequel, Aliens, couldn't rely on graphic strangeness to sell a now-known quantity? Not entirely. What had to work now was dictated by certain givens. One given was Sigourney Weaver. She became a bigger star than the original villain, the alien. A unique symbol could be made of her, female as hero. How did you make her look like a hero? By the juxtaposition of two symbols. A female with a gun. Fighting the forces of evil. It was a variation on a wartime recruitment poster with a woman as the soldier. But was this enough? Wasn't something missing? S t r a n g e n e s s ? U n e a r t h l i n e s s ? Vulnerability? Yes. Something to help the audience identify with a victim – a victim of the terror brought about by this horrific alien. In this lay the promise of a thrilling movie – the thrill of the struggle of the victim against the alien. Sigourney Weaver, with an attitude, with a gun, certainly didn't look like a victim. Borrowing from Eisenstein, I put a child in jeopardy, put that child in Weaver's arms. The child had to be totally terrified. Woman? Gun? Child? Joan of Arc. *Liberté*. *Égalité*. *Fraternité*. The symbols of the French Revolution, that kind of moving symbolism. Symbol, too, of the feminist revolution. Yes. The only missing piece now was strangeness. That unearthly quality. The identity of the first 'ALIEN', that graphic symbolism of weirdness. The egg. What did you create for the genre effect in this sequel? A nest of eggs of aliens. Sigourney Weaver, a child, a gun, in a nest of alien eggs? It worked. 'ALIENS' was the highest grossing film of the 'ALIENS' trilogy. But, as they say in the movie biz, what have you done lately? 'Jurassic Park', 'Blown Away', 'Legends of the Fall', 'Basic Instinct', 'Bugsy', 'The Shadow', 'Tank Girl', 'Cable Guy'; these are all motion picture ad campaigns, film and print, that I've helped with on since 'ALIENS'.

"So much of what we create for entertainment is

derivative, it helps to have a library of visual

communication histories in your head.

That comes only from education. Self education.

School education. Awareness."

"Successful movie work has a million authors. We've created

lot of success only to have someone else finish our work."

THEY'RE REAL!
D TRY: "THEY ARE REAL!"
HERE THEY ARE REAL!"
HERE DINOSAURS ARE REAL"
3 DIFFERENT TAG LINES

JURASSIC

JURASSIC PARK

"Spielberg simply wanted a badge. An icon trapped in

shape that would be universally merchandisable..."

> **I've always taken jobs just a rag, Levi's had done dumb dinosaur movie.**

ryone else said were dead ends — 'Rolling Stone' was
eir best advertising, and this was just another

Illustrations by Terry Lamb.

MOONSTRUCK

CHER · NICOLAS CAGE

METRO-GOLDWYN-MAYER PRESENTS A PATRICK PALMER-NORMAN JEWISON PRODUCTION

A NORMAN JEWISON FILM

"MOONSTRUCK" STARRING VINCENT GARDENIA OLYMPIA DUKAKIS AND DANNY AIELLO MUSIC COMPOSED AND ADAPTED BY DICK HYMAN

PRODUCTION DESIGNER PHILIP ROSENBERG COSTUME DESIGNER THEONI V. ALDREDGE DIRECTOR OF PHOTOGRAPHY DAVID WATKIN FILM EDITOR LOU LOMBARDO

ASSOCIATE PRODUCER BONNIE PALEF WRITTEN BY JOHN PATRICK SHANLEY PRODUCED BY PATRICK PALMER & NORMAN JEWISON

DIRECTED BY NORMAN JEWISON

PG PARENTAL GUIDANCE SUGGESTED
SOME MATERIAL MAY NOT BE SUITABLE FOR CHILDREN

DOLBY STEREO

© 1987 METRO-GOLDWYN-MAYER PICTURES INC.

He has everything at stake.
He can't afford to lose.
He's got to make all the right moves.

TOM CRUISE
ALL THE Right Moves

It isn't the Bronx or Brooklyn, it isn't even New York.
It's Chinatown... and it's about to explode.

A MICHAEL CIMINO FILM

YEAR OF THE DRAGON

Enter a world beyond your wildest imagination where anything can happen.

DREAMSCAPE

Close your eyes and the adventure begins.

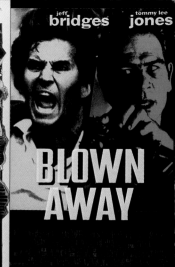

jeff bridges   tommy lee jones

BLOWN AWAY

NO COWBOYS, NO INDIANS,
NO CAVALRY TO THE RESCUE,
ONLY A COP.

PAUL NEWMAN in
FORT APACHE,
THE BRONX

Mickey Spillane's
I, THE JURY

FROM THE MAKERS OF SINBAD IN SPECTACULAR DYNARAMA
THE INCREDIBLE SEARCH THAT BECAME
THE MOST EXCITING LEGEND OF ALL.

JASON
AND THE ARGONAUTS

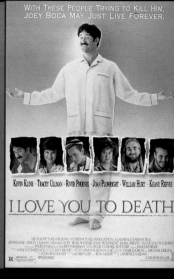

WITH THESE PEOPLE TRYING TO KILL HIM,
JOEY BOCA MAY JUST LIVE FOREVER.

KEVIN KLINE · TRACEY ULLMAN · RIVER PHOENIX · JOAN PLOWRIGHT · WILLIAM HURT · KEANU REEVES

I LOVE YOU TO DEATH

He sold his
soul for
rock 'n' roll.

Aunt Felice has a
nasty way of
showing her
affection...

THE KISS
Don't do it
with your eyes closed.

The marketing exec said she wanted a concept for a poster – not a layout. I asked her, since she was obviously more aquainted with the visual arts than me, to show me examples of each so I could learn.
Pointing to a poster with two big heads over a skyline she said "that is a concept, an idea."
The 'Aliens' poster, which I felt was one of the best visual metaphors we ever created for a movie, she told me, closing her eyes was "simply a layout".

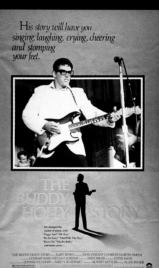

His story will have you
singing, laughing, crying, cheering
and stomping
your feet.

THE BUDDY HOLLY STORY

Follow
the newest
cat-and-creature
game
as played
through

STEPHEN KING'S
Cat's Eye

Blame it on RIO

GREYSTOKE

THE LEGEND OF TARZAN LORD OF THE APES

Only One Man Could Dazzle Hollywood,
Charm The World's Women,
And Turn A Dust Bowl
Into A Glittering Paradise.

bugsy

"

Here is our rough of the Flamingo Hotel reflected in Bugsy's shiny shoes because the studio told us to be different. We created things we thought were different for a movie poster. Then after our presentation, the studio thanked us very much and someone else was put on the job ...why? I was told we were just toooo different even though they did use one of our concepts later.

They Say The West Is The Land Of Opportunity.
For Bugsy Siegel,
That Was An Understatement.

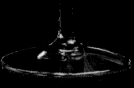
Bugsy

Be prolific.

Be fast.

At the time, 'Greystoke' was the most expensive presentation ever made for a movie campaign. Each concept was a finished piece of art.

bugsy

Or don't do movie work."

'To Live and Die in L.A.' was a film I asked to work on and it was one of the few that I worked very hard at selling the concept I felt was right...
My client, Greg Morrison, believed me and helped make it better.

A Federal Agent is dead.
A killer is loose.
And the City of Angels
is about to explode.

The director of
"The French Connection"
is back on the street again...

Save those rejects. You never know... ”

Like a scary drug, a good idea should have a long, vivid half life. You can use the flashbacks forever.

Bugsy

Most People Saw Nothing But A Dustbowl In The Middle Of The Desert.

One Man Saw A Palace Glittering With Lights And Ringing With The Sound Of Money.

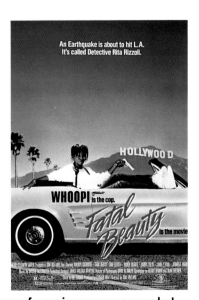

An Earthquake is about to hit L.A. It's called Detective Rita Rizzoli.

HOLLYWOOD

WHOOPI is the cop.
Fatal Beauty is the movie.

Brad Pitt, Warren Beatty and Whoopie Goldberg as James Dean. A lawyer would call the use of a previous success a precedent.

"MOTION PICTURE ADS USUALLY TAKE A LONG TRIP TO COME BACK TO THE BEGINNING CONCEPT."

...anyone?

JIM CARREY   MATTHEW BRODERICK

There's no such thing
as free cable.

THE
CABLE
GUY

Finished art: Aspect Ratio

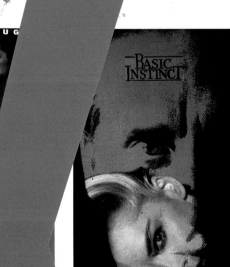
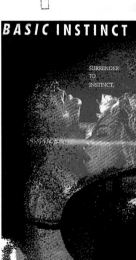

"SEX SELLS."

Sex is like pizza even at it's worst it's still good."

A brutal murder.

A brilliant killer.

A cop who can't

resist the danger.

BASIC INSTINCT

MICHAEL DOUGLAS   KATHLEEN TURNER   DANNY DE VITO

Romancing The STONE

She's a girl from the big city.
He's a reckless soldier of fortune.
For a fabulous treasure,
they share an adventure
no one could imagine...
or survive.

TWENTIETH CENTURY FOX presents A MICHAEL DOUGLAS PRODUCTION A ROBERT ZEMECKIS FILM
MICHAEL DOUGLAS KATHLEEN TURNER ROMANCING THE STONE starring DANNY DE VITO ALFONSO ARAU MANUEL OJEDA
production design by LAWRENCE G. PAULL director of photography DEAN CUNDEY music by ALAN SILVESTRI written by DIANE THOMAS
produced by MICHAEL DOUGLAS directed by ROBERT ZEMECKIS

A movie has

no shelf life

if it doesn't make it

The most often used movie poster design strategy is to show the merchandize for sale – the actors – in an environmemt that promises an exotic locale with other symbolic elements in place that hint at the story promise – or as we like to call it "two big heads over a skyline with sex or violence or laughs".

Like every magazine cover or book cover, record cover or software package – every movie poster has a distinctly recognizable format that says to the customer this is legit – the real thing.

TWO CHILDREN
ORPHANS IN A LUSH
TROPICAL PARADISE
UNFAMILIAR WITH THEIR SEX
OR THEIR CIVILIZATION,
AWAKEN TO EACH OTHER
WITH CONFUSION, JOY AND
A NATURAL FULFILLMENT

on day one

it's dead meat

There was no clear marketing strategy for something as different as 'Rumblefish' – so two campaigns were produced and printed – one illustrated and one photographic. When that didn't work, the illustrated version was recreated photographically.

!

OVER 300 MOVIES A

ID STILL COUNTING...

It was my first commercial, my idea, my art, my copy, my

ENGLISH TOFFEE

(MUSIC)

Announcer
first time i

Shrink-to-fit 501s... now in
the Junior Department from
Levi's Womenswear.

to fit every curve... like no
denim you've ever worn.

WOMA
year to

GOTCHA

In 1979 the Levi's spot cost $250,000. In 1985 four Gotcha

dit, me, me, me.

e: For the
tory,

Levi's shrink-to-fit, button fly,
501 Jeans

are cut especially for women.
In the only shrinking denim,
that "tailors" itself in the wash,

QUALITY NEVER GOES OUT OF STYLE.

(WIND)
LOGO

ravis, you're a
e!"

spots cost only $80,000. Welcome to the computer age.

" MY 'ROCKY'
HIGHEST
WITH

ROCKY IV

GET READY FOR
THE NEXT WORLD WAR

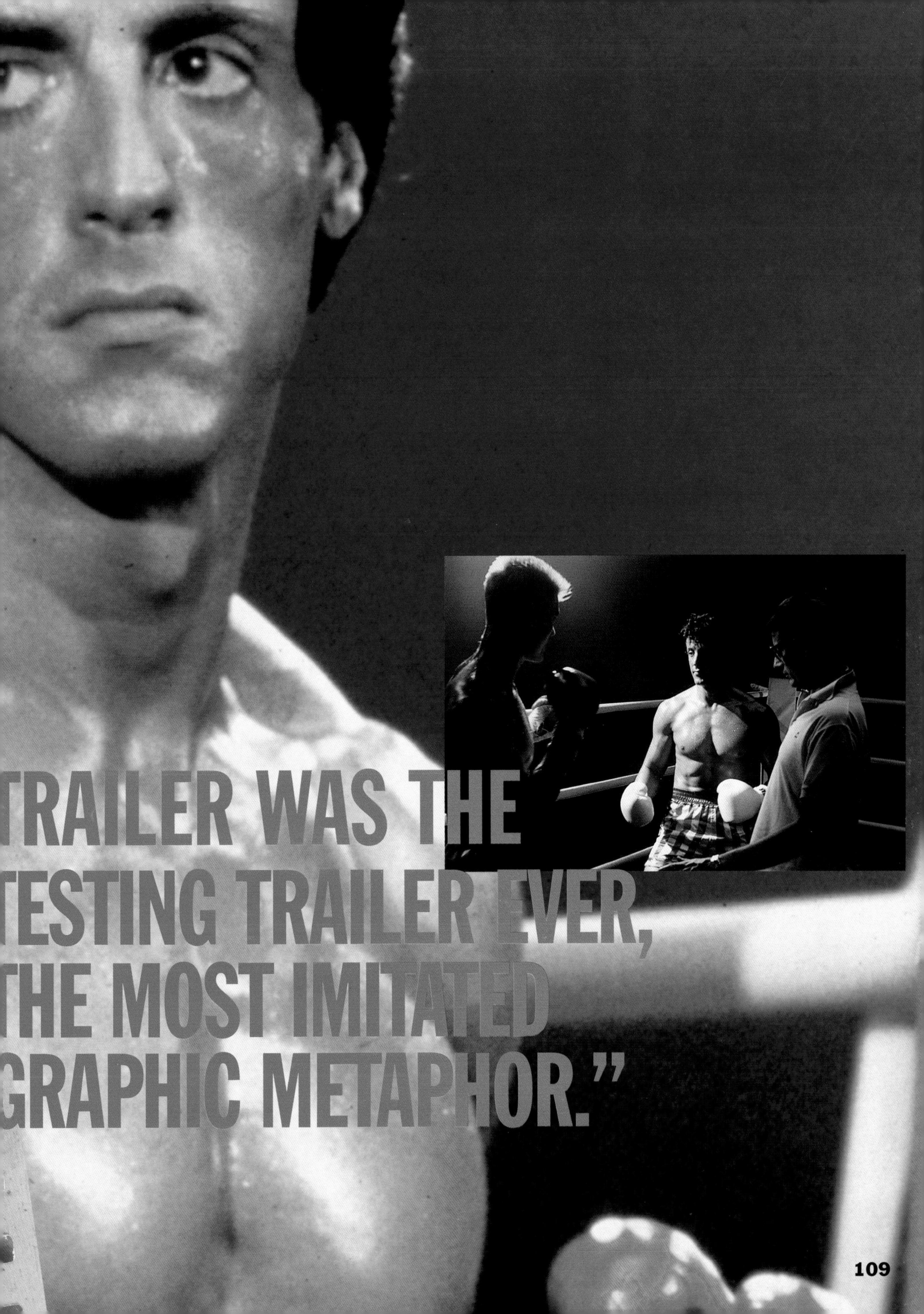

TRAILER WAS THE
TESTING TRAILER EVER,
THE MOST IMITATED
GRAPHIC METAPHOR."

We've seen it in Bud Bowls. We've seen it on Monday night football… we've seen head thumpin', battle thumpin', anything thumpin' everywhere. Yet you say you were the first? Yes, with the exploding boxing gloves I created for the 'Rocky IV' advertising campaign. **You blew up two boxing gloves? Why?** I needed a dynamic ending for the live action footage I created and directed for the trailers and TV spots. I needed a symbol on the move. **Is Stallone really that short?** He only looks that short because of the way I positioned him up against Dolph Lundgren – the Russian boxer. **So you made Dolph look bigger than Rocky… is that all?** To give them even more symbolism Rocky wore red, white and blue… Dolph wore Soviet red. Rocky's gloves were white, Dolph's red. **Isn't the live footage all clips from the feature?** No. I shot all of that new. I had them both preparing for the night… meeting in the ring – then they each took a swing at the other. **Red glove meets white glove? And kablooey!!! Did anyone get their hand hurt?** No. The gloves that exploded were plaster replicas. We matched the shot of the replicas to the last frame of the live gloves right before they collided. **Was this branding?** Yes, we encapsulated the essence of the film in a small space. Using a visual metaphor we created by combining two symbols – the red glove and the American glove – we used that space to leverage a look, a feel, and to create a dynamic presentation. **Did it work?** Yes, 'Rocky IV' was the highest grossing in ticket sales of all the 'Rocky' movies.

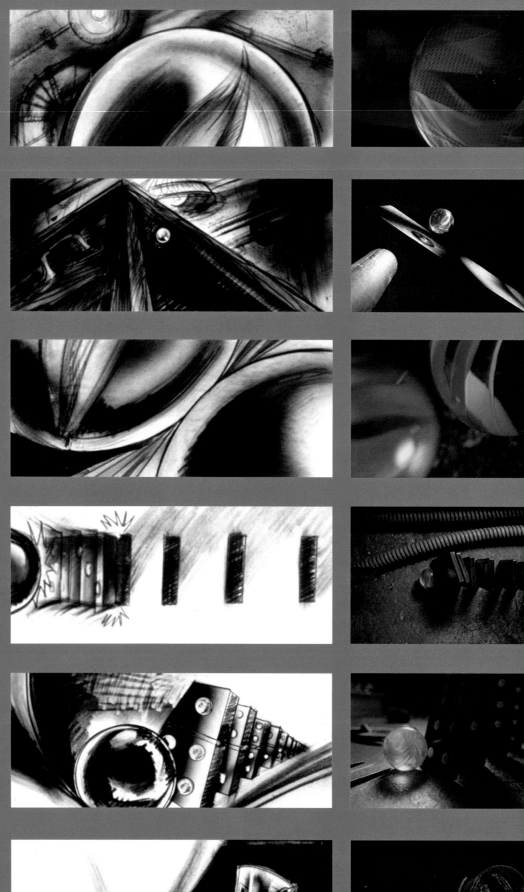

"Always refer to the **story**

Jeff Bridges

JEFF BRIDGES

Tommy Lee Jones

TOMMY LEE JONES

B L O W N
A W A Y

BLOWN
AWAY

Know what the picture will look like
boards. before shooting."

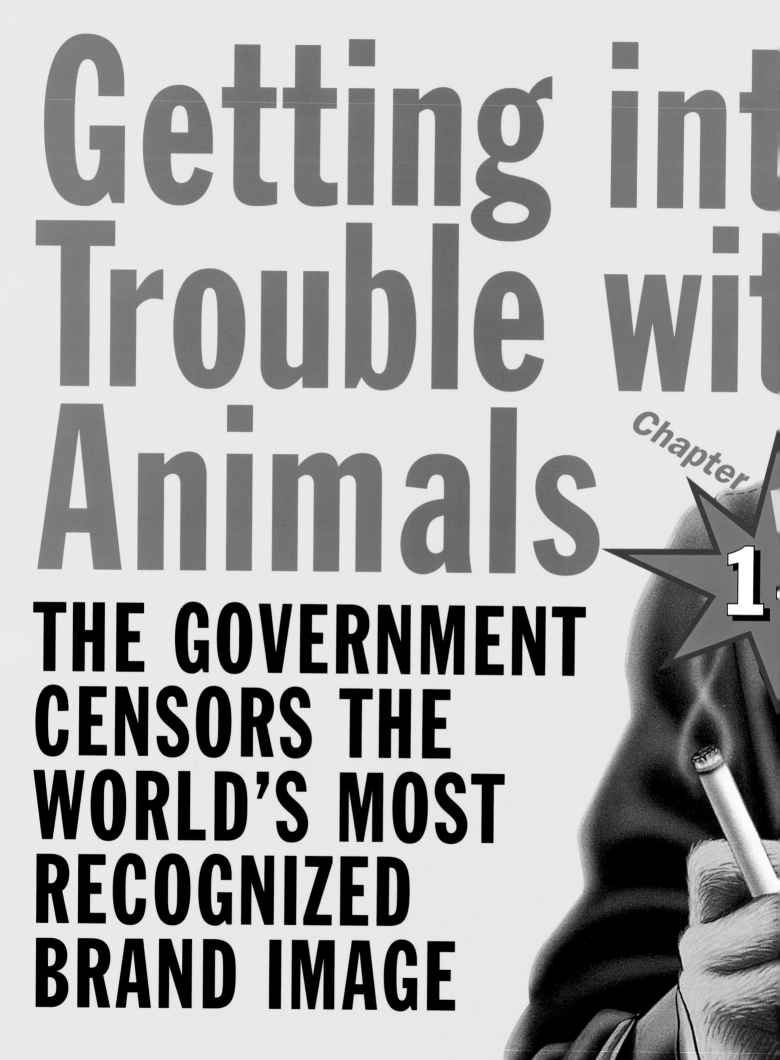

Getting int[o] Trouble wit[h] Animals

THE GOVERNMENT CENSORS THE WORLD'S MOST RECOGNIZED BRAND IMAGE

JOE CAMEL

Where did 'Joe Camel' come from? Camel needed a new image, stronger and more memorable than the Marlboro Man. Marlboro was the number one package goods brand in the world. Its image was one of the most recognised in the world, ranking right up there with Coca-Cola and Mickey Mouse. Camel needed a symbol to match the Marlboro cowboy. **But McCann Ericson, one of the biggest ad agencies in the world had the Camel account. How did Mike Salisbury of area code 310 shoot down the Marlboro cowboy?** The agency's original concept was to recreate motion picture advertising that recalled memorable characters whose personality was created partly by a cigarette smoking. Bogart-like detectives, WWII pilots, merchant seamen, soldiers of fortune – anything but cowboys. **You left out animals.** Besides film and print entertainment advertising; 'Rocky IV', 'Aliens', 'Jurassic Park', I created a lot of magazine design. 'Playboy', 'West', 'Surfer', 'Surfing', 'City', 'Sassy', 'Hot Rod'. For some of those magazines I also produced articles introducing illustrative nostalgia and popular culture subjects. I created the first articles on the art of Coca-Cola, Mickey Mouse, California custom cars, orange crate labels and movie posters. My magazine work revived airbrush illustration, and my illustration concepts for album covers were nominated for Grammies. One is in the permanent collection of the Smithsonian. **OK. The agency felt your background gave you the experience and insight to select the exact right style of illustration for the nostalgia look Camel wanted. And to style the look correctly to fit this movie concept. So what happened?** That concept, the old time movie poster look, did not test well with the target. **Who was that target?** People over 25 who were already smokers. **Mike, with the failure of the nostalgia look to appeal to the target, how did you create an image, a symbol, just plain old advertising that could beat the biggest selling brand in the world?** It was almost inevitable that in developing a character to be the brand-symbol for Camel that an actual camel would be used. So over the body of my billboard mock-up illustration of a forties Philip Marlowe private eye character, in trench coat with slouch, I pasted the head of a camel. **So this was 'Joe'?** Not yet. He went into the garbage. However, I later pulled it out, thinking, not entirely bad. I had always been creating high-concept images, combining two known symbols to create a new communication. **A visual metaphor?** I did this for award-winning magazine covers, for example, the CBS eye with a teardrop to symbolize the end of the 'Ed Sullivan Show', a skull with red lips, to say 'Smack!' I put San Francisco preserved in a mason jar. **High-concept communication.** People get it. They may not get fancy designs or esoteric decoration, but they know good ideas. I said "this too is high concept; let's test it". **And?** It failed the test. **I ask again, where did 'Joe' come from?** The concept didn't fail; the idea of a realistic camel in surreal surroundings got the target's attention. It was the nostalgia that failed. So I brought Joe into the 20th century. **I see that you gave Joe an Armani blazer with a colored t-shirt, spiked his hair, put on Ray-Bans, gave him a Corvette dressed with a starlet perched on the hood and parked it in front of the Hollywood sign?** Yes. To speak to the target, I had to make 'Joe' cool. And I did it in day-glo colors. **Why day-glo?** Each element of the illustration had its own distinct bright color. That way, each symbol would read when seen at 65 miles per hour. **What were these elements?** I work in the magic of threes. **Magic?** Groups of three – eat, drink, be merry; stop, look and listen – are memorable. I designed the boards with three symbols. **Bingo?** It tested out of the ballpark. But he still needed personality. He needed to be able to express himself. **Is he a penis?** No, he is Sean Connery. **Sean Connery?** Yes. He didn't have hands and he couldn't change his expression. I didn't know how Joe could express different attitudes so I searched for a feature that he could talk with. **And?** It was James Bond's eyebrows. **You created 'Joe'.** A visual brand metaphor more powerful than words. A picture of the brand's identity. More importantly, this is a perfect brand symbol. Nothing is borrowed. The consumer does not need to search his vocabulary of symbols to solve the communication. It says what the product is. **You mean you could run a 'Joe Camel' ad and never have to show a pack, or a word that says Camel?** 'Joe'. And so I created 'Joe Camel' advertising, 'Joe Camel' outdoor, 'Joe Camel' promotions, 'Joe Camel' merchandize, 'Joe Camel' packaging. I created ads and merchandizing for Camel-sponsored motor racing events. **Didn't Camel increase market share at the expense of Marlboro?** Yes. Marlboro is desperately trying illustration, promotions, even price-cutting to compete. **Who would have thought a camel could out-draw a macho cowboy?** Who would have thought a brand image would have increased sales 1000%?

Mike is an earth-shattering, powerful designer of important imagery. 'Joe Camel' is only a piece of his career... Mike has done wonderful design for all kinds of people.

Paula Scher
Pentagram Design, New York

THERE'S STILL ONE WITH CHAR

9 mg. "tar", 1.2 mg. nicotine av. per cigarette by FTC method.

"This is where we started... reviving dead movie icons who smoked Camels as part of their character..."

"The problem with nostalgia is that the ta

16 mg. "tar", 1.2 mg. nicotine av. per cigarette by FTC method.

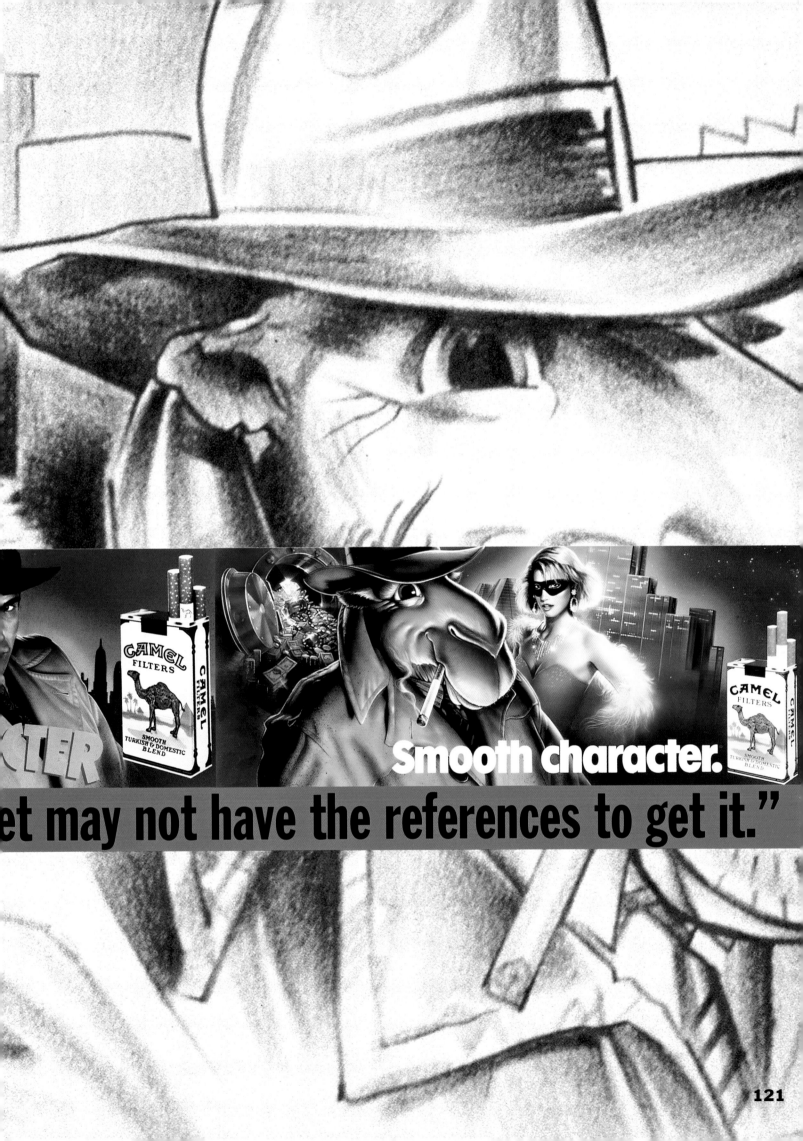

121

"TOLD TO CREATE A SYMBOL MORE POWERFUL THAN THE COWBOY... WE DID."

After we did all of our visual
research, several pencils were
created, then a color rough was
prepared using a palette Pat Linse
devised for each illustration.
Several illustrators would be involved
in the finish, each chosen for their
particular field of expertise: a car
person did the car, a body person for
the body, there was even a head
specialist we called Deep Throat.

"SOMETIMES A CIGARET

IS JUST A CIGARETTE."

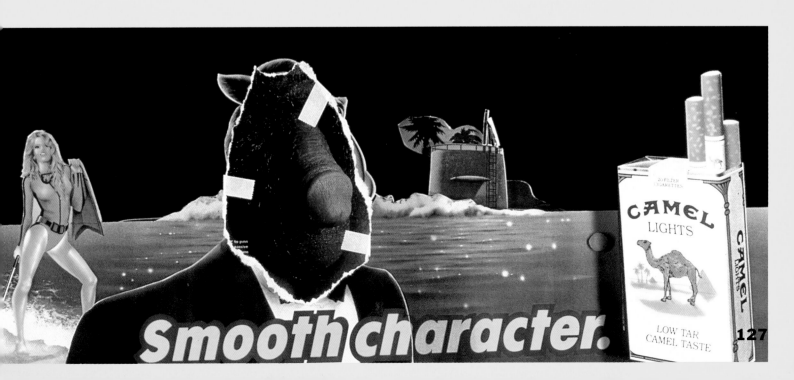

smooth character.

We proudly introduce the most imitated logo on earth.

See? You're imitating it right now. And you're not even
playing Monopoly or Star Wars or Mr. Potato Head or
G.I Joe, or with Nerf balls or Tonka Trucks.

But you have, and you will.

And every time they make you smile, if you look closely,
you'll see our smile grow just a little brighter.

LOGOS
BRAND
IDENTITY

If in the business of communications, 'Image is king,' the essence of this image, the logo, is the jewel in its crown. **"** **Paul Rand**

HASBRO

TM

"Hasbro makes toys, toys are fun, fun makes people smile."

MICHAEL
MANN
PRODUCTIONS

Blue Note

What is a PolyGram? It's an established worldwide record label – PolyGram Records is a giant collective of five music labels. **What did you do for them?** I created a corporate identity for this new company with the old funny name. **PolyGram is based in New York, Mike Salisbury is in California, why did they come to you?** They heard about my brand identity programs for Blue Note Records, United Artist Records, Bertlesman, A&M, and RCA – major music entities. **O.K., Big question. Isn't a polygram a many-sided figure? And why is there no polygram in the PolyGram logo?** The president of PolyGram is an art collector and he wanted something less mechanical than a literal polygram... he wanted something more expressionistic. I created a visual metaphor for him. We composed a P with a G clef – **What made this logo expressionistic?** We painted the logo with a brush, much like Japanese calligraphy, which is very loose but at the same time extremely urgent – the essence of expressionism. **O.K. It's now a musical logo. It's now expressionistic. What makes it a brand?** The entire communications system of stationery, company literature, packaging, and signage is woven together with consistent typography we designed to give the logo a respectable business suit. This made PolyGram unique and fresh enough to stand out in a crowded industry, and rooted and polished enough to be comfortable in a business environment. **Is there a Mike Salisbury method to successful brand building?** It's all about being appropriate and consistent. Meeting the client's needs takes a front seat in the creative process at Salisbury. We build a logo, a brand, an identity around what each client wants to accomplish. **Form definately follows function.**

PACKAGING

ubbleYum

®
5 PIECES/BUBBLE GUM

bleYum

®
5 PIECES/BUBBLE GUM

ar

ubbleYum

®
5 PIECES/BUBBLE GUM

elon

HALO

HALO

HALO

HALO

HALO

HALO

halo

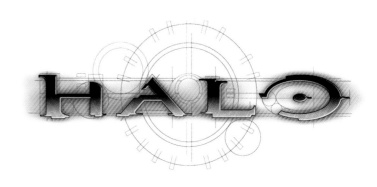

options,
we give clients options.
It's a proactive business —
our clients are our partners..."

"Kirin wanted an American-looking beer. I gambled with **green.** In Japan they like green.

"There isn't a package more sexy than a black leather jacket unzipped."

The New South Coast Plaza.

SOUTH
COAST
PLAZA

"We were doing a lot of surf stuff at the tim

You packaged air? And beer. And software. And liquor. And clothing, videos, games, tapes, soup, potato chips, records. **What brands?** Mattel, Kirin, TDK, Nintendo, Software Ventures, Gotcha, O.P., Suntory, Nalleys, Andersons. **Let's get to the packaging air part.** Bubble Yum was losing a lot of share to Bubbliscious. Their agency came to me to stop the losses. **How do you do that?** Gum is purchased in stores on racks. I've been successful selling magazines, records, and videos off racks. The gum wasn't the problem. **What was the problem?** Their packaging was silent. **Silent?** Too quiet. Kids are raised on noisy back-lit pictures with bright colors. **TV? Video games?** And they don't respond to dull packages on dingy racks in dimly lit corner Mom & Pops. **Moms & Pops.** Whatever. **So, tell us, what was the solution?** Day-glo. I didn't have electricity to light up the package, so I used bright day-glo colors. I had previously used day-glo to light up a whole culture. **Culture?** Surfing. I redesigned 'Surfing Magazine' and reintroduced day-glo with rip and tear and slash graphics to the world. **There you go again. That, I invented the whole world hyperbole.** It worked for ad campaigns I created too. **Hype?** No, day-glo. **I know, the day-glo posters you created for the movie 'Blown Away'.** And don't forget my Back to the Beach campaign and Joe Camel. All done with day-glo. It's a very useful tool. **You can even package air with it?**

Mattel wanted us to adapt the surf OOstyle to a game."

MIKE'S PIX

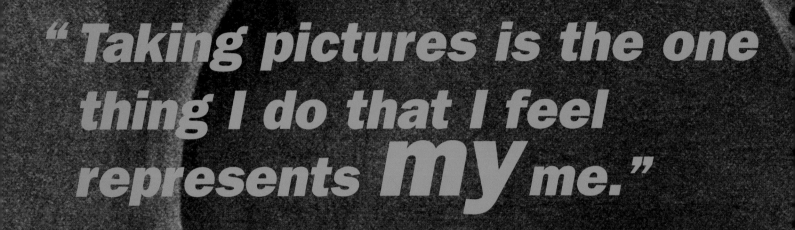

"**Taking pictures is the one thing I do that I feel represents** my **me.**"

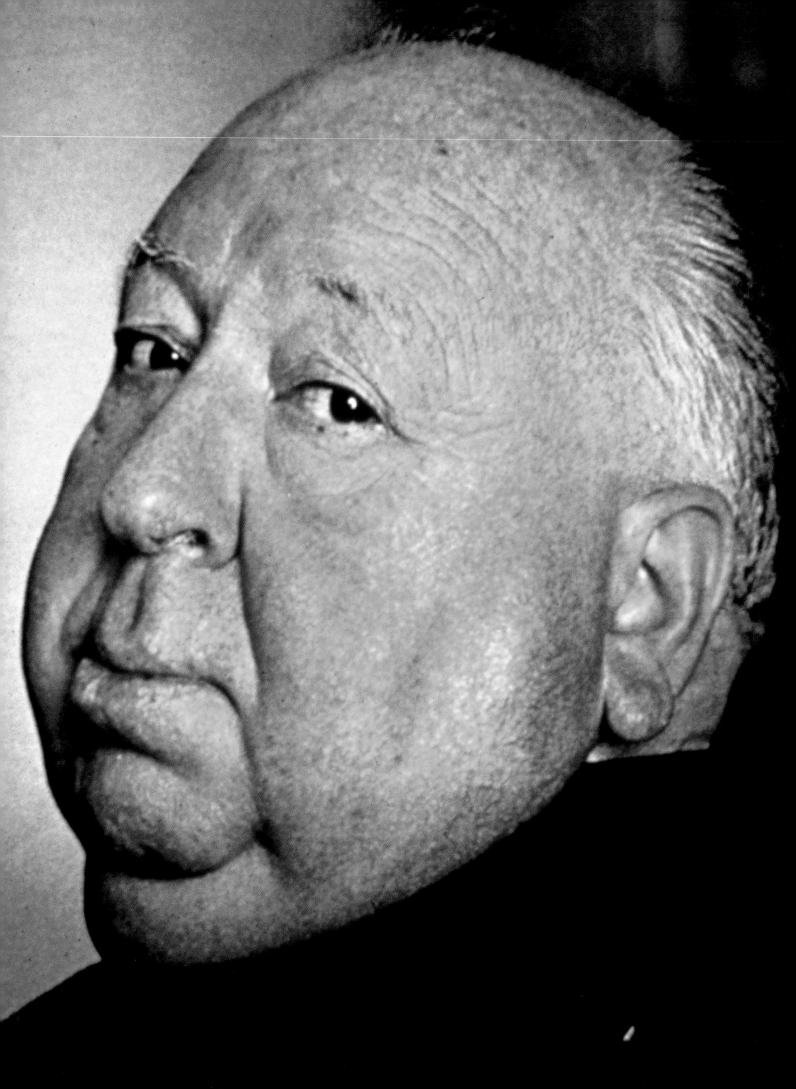

Credits:

Scott Binkley
Tony Davis
Sarah Dombrowsky
Anja Duering
Dave Goodman
Regina Grosvald
Allana Lee
Sjoerd Liefting
Pat Linse
Suzanne Mantell
Maryevelyn McGough
Tor Naerheim
Kate Noël-Paton
Tanya Presby
The Sanders
Dwight Smith
Jim Wojtowicz